Clare's Kitchen

Clare's Kitchen

THE ALL-PARTY COOKBOOK

CLARE LATIMER

BLOOMSBURY

First published in Great Britain 1994
Bloomsbury Publishing Limited, 2 Soho Square, London W1V 5DE

Copyright © 1994 by Clare Latimer

The moral right of the author has been asserted

Photography by Julie Dixon
Line illustrations by John Hannay

A CIP catalogue record for this book
is available from the British Library

ISBN 0 7475 1704 5

10   9   8   7   6   5   4   3   2   1

Edited by Susan Conder
Designed by Fielding Rowinski
Typeset by Hewer Text Composition Services, Edinburgh
Printed and bound in Great Britain by
Butler & Tanner Ltd, Frome and London

To Theo Cowan, the great eater and PR man,
who died on my birthday in 1991

My thanks to my mum for getting me interested in good food,
to Donald and Diana Sinden for starting me off on large parties,
to Lord and Lady Walker for their consistent support
and to Zoe Jackson for being my other pair of hands

Contents

Introduction

My feeling is that not many people read this part of a cookbook, so I shall make it brief and, I hope, worthy of your time.

I have run an outside catering company now for twenty years and decided to share our popular and well-tried recipes. I never had catering training, but my mum cooks well and I have always had a keen interest in eating well. There is a great cross-section of recipes from old-fashioned steamed puddings to modern combinations such as avocado served on a strawberry purée. A lot of the standard recipes have personal touches, such as adding a beaten egg white to lemon meringue pie filling to lighten its texture. Tips like this come from cooking the same recipes over and over again, aiming for perfection.

This book shows you how to entertain on your own. I accept that not everyone can cook to professional standards, but if you are keen and enjoy eating then this book will suit you. I have coded each recipe with a symbol for easy (🥄), moderately demanding (🥄🥄) and challenging (🥄🥄🥄), so you can start with the easy, foolproof recipes and then progress to harder ones. I also suggest menus at the beginning of the book, but my best tip for choosing a menu is to cook what *you* feel like eating that day. So many people choose what they *think* their guests would like and this can so often go wrong for all sorts of reasons – not least the weather!

There are only a few things I feel very strongly about. Freshly ground black pepper is a must. It adds a special flavour and is a good garnish to many dishes. It is said – and I, too, believe – that Italians have the healthiest diet in the world; this is partly due to their lavish use of oils. Good oils can change a very ordinary dish into something special, so where I mention good olive and nut oils, DO NOT cheat and use cheap ones. Nutmeg should always be freshly ground and this should not present a problem: just make sure you always have a whole nut ready to grate in the cupboard. I keep one in a nutmeg grinder, which helps prevent grated fingertips!

I have also indicated on each recipe whether the dish can be frozen. This is useful if you are busy and also trying to entertain, but frozen cooked dishes should not be kept more than a week or two as the real fresh flavour vanishes, especially with puddings.

Good luck with this book – but please don't become too successful or I will be out of a job!

CLARE LATIMER

EVERY KITCHEN SHOULD HAVE ...

1 large, non-stick frying pan

1 non-stick omelette pan

3 large saucepans with lids

2 medium saucepans with lids

1 small, non-stick saucepan

1 measuring jug

3 plastic mixing bowls

1 baby nylon sieve

1 large nylon sieve

1 grater

1 large casserole dish

2 medium casserole dishes

2 small casserole dishes

1 whisk

2 plastic spatulas

1 hand whisk or electric hand whisk

1 rolling pin

1 pair scissors

2 wooden spoons

1 piping bag with set of nozzles

1 baking tray

salt and pepper grinders

nutmeg grinder

herb rack

1 lemon squeezer

2 or more cake tins

1 colander

1 small, sharp knife

1 medium, sharp knife

1 fish knife

1 large, sharp knife

1 carving knife and fork

1 bread knife

1 knife sharpener

1 small palette knife

1 large, plastic, heat-proof palette knife

1 draining spoon

2 large spoons

1 soup ladle

1 potato masher

1 potato peeler

1 potato brush

4 patty tins with 12 cups in each tray

1 electric blender

HANDY HINTS

To keep prepared potatoes white, put into a bowl of cold water with a slice of lemon.

To cut very thin slices of bread, put the loaf into the deep freeze, spread with butter and then cut each slice.

If you do not eat much bread, buy a fresh loaf, slice and freeze in an airtight bag. Take out one slice at a time; it will thaw in a few minutes or toast immediately.

Sprinkle caster sugar over custard or lay clingfilm over the surface to prevent skin forming.

To prevent skin forming on white sauce, pour over the last tablespoon of milk. Before serving, reheat gently, stirring in the rest of the milk.

Run cooked green vegetables under cold water to retain good colour.

To keep watercress fresh, put leaf ends into a bowl of water.

To cut pastry off the top of an uncooked tart, roll the rolling pin over the top.

If you use tinned tomato purée, freeze the excess in ice cube trays, taking out a cube when needed.

Chop up any excess fresh herbs and keep in airtight bags in the deep freeze.

Add a little bicarbonate of soda to green vegetables when cooking (and rinse in cold water when cooked), to enhance their green colour.

To measure butter, score light marks on the surface.

To measure treacle, stand the tin on the scales and spoon out the amount needed, deducting the weight. This saves wasting treacle and saves on washing up.

Freeze pint cartons of milk, or half pints if you live alone.

Make odd ends of bread into breadcrumbs and freeze.

Add a dessertspoon of red wine to a small tin of baked beans to get a 'posh' vegetable!

Cocktail Parties

Giving a cocktail party is an easy way to entertain a group of friends without too much work. Although the food can be quite fiddly to make, there is very little clearing up to do after everyone has gone. A great deal can be done in advance and frozen. I have mentioned cocktail sticks in recipes that require them – it's surprisingly easy to remember all the ingredients and then suddenly find you've nothing to stick them on.

Quantities are generous and simple: five or six different choices, and two of each item per person, i.e. twelve mouthfuls each. If your friends are eating out after the party you can cut down. I also serve two dips with crudités at each party; these add a fresh taste and are good for dieters.

Drinks can be kept simple by restricting the choice. My favourite idea is to serve straight Champagne or sparkling wine or offer Champagne Cocktail (a sugar lump in each glass with a teaspoon of brandy, topped up with Champagne), Sunset Strip (one-third apricot juice and two-thirds Champagne) or Black Velvet (one-third Guinness and two-thirds Champagne). This way, you don't have to overstock on each choice of drink, and the glasses are easy to refill as it is clear what each person has been drinking. Allow half a bottle of wine per person unless it is going to be a wild party. Most off-licences do sale or return and will usually lend glasses.

Here are a few menus for you with contrasting tastes and textures, a guide to difficulty of preparation and the items that can be frozen – generally these take a long time to make, so think well in advance.

Suggested Cocktail-Party Menus

Quick and Easy

SMOKED SALMON WITH AVOCADO	COCKTAIL SAUSAGES WITH CHUTNEY
STUFFED MUSHROOMS	VARIOUS VOL-AU-VENTS
MELON AND MANGO CHEESES	CREAM CHEESE AND CHUTNEY DIP
	CRISPS

Easy But Not So Quick

TOMATO, MOZZARELLA AND BLACK OLIVE KEBABS	TURKEY-STUFFING MEATBALLS WITH CRANBERRY DIP
STUFFED DATES WITH CREAM CHEESE AND ORANGE	CROQUE MONSIEUR
	FRIED BREAKFAST KEBABS
GOAT-CHEESE AND STRAWBERRY TARTLETS	ROQUEFORT DIP WITH CRUDITÉS

Completely Frozen and Plated

The following can be arranged and frozen on hardy dinner plates, and brought out about six hours before serving. This is a wonderful way to entertain, and you will enjoy the food the more for having had a break before eating. Warm all except the smoked salmon whirls in a very low oven and then garnish with parsley sprigs or other herbs, such as dill.

BARBECUED MEATBALLS	SMOKED SALMON WHIRLS
ROLL-UP BACON IDEAS	CHEESE STRAWS (STORED, NOT FROZEN)
TOAD-IN-THE-HOLE	

Quite Time-Consuming But Half Freezer-Friendly

I have asterisked the parts of the canapés that can be frozen; the rest can be done on the day.

BLUEBERRY MUFFINS* WITH SMOKED MACKEREL MOUSSE	YORKSHIRE PUDS* WITH RARE ROAST BEEF
BLINIS* WITH SMOKED SALMON AND SOURED CREAM	BABY HAMBURGERS*
	CHOUX BALLS* WITH STILTON AND PORT

Very Time-Consuming But Really Impressive

SMOKED SALMON AND SPINACH ROULADE	SCRAMBLED EGGS AND ANCHOVY TOASTIES
MARINATED HERRINGS AND PEARS WITH SOURED CREAM	PEKING DUCK
QUAIL EGGS WITH BACON	BLUEBERRY MUFFINS
	SMOKED MUSSEL DIP WITH CRUDITÉS

RECIPES

Avocado Dip

If you like hot food, be generous with the grated onion and Tabasco; if not, just use the amount stated in the recipe. Prepare this on the day of the party, otherwise it discolours.

1 ripe avocado
*225 g	8 oz cream cheese*
juice of ½ lemon
1 tsp grated onion
1 tsp Worcestershire sauce
a dash of Tabasco
1 tbsp double cream
salt and freshly ground black pepper

Halve the avocado, remove the stone and scoop out the flesh. Put all the ingredients into a blender and whizz until smooth. Place in a small bowl, cover with clingfilm and chill.

MAKES 3 RAMEKINS / ♦

Cream Cheese and Chutney Dip

So simple and good for people with a sweet tooth. Try varying the flavour with other chutneys or plum sauce.

*225 g	8 oz cream cheese*
1 tbsp mango chutney

Blend together until smooth, put into a dish and chill.

♦

Smoked Mussel Dip

Very impressive, easy and an unusual exotic flavour. A good change from taramasalata.

1 × 105 g / 4 oz tin of smoked mussels
225 g / 8 oz cream cheese
a dash of Tabasco
freshly ground black pepper
1 tsp grated onion (optional)

Put all ingredients including the mussel oil into a blender and mix until smooth. Put into a dish and chill.

Roquefort Dip

Depending on the consistency of the cream cheese, you may like to add a little milk to soften the mixture.

125 g / 4 oz Roquefort cheese
225 g / 8 oz cream cheese
a little milk, if required

Put all ingredients into a blender and mix until smooth. Put into a dish and chill.

Serve any of the above dips with prepared, bite-sized crudités, such as raw cauliflower florets, carrots, button mushrooms, celery, radish, peppers (various colours), courgettes, spring onions, cherry tomatoes and broccoli florets. Pitta bread and crisps can also be served.

Ham Round Brie

Make these simple, fresh-tasting canapés on the day of the party. Use slightly under-ripe Brie, ideally British such as Somerset, and keep the canapés in the dark until ready to serve, as ham discolours in light. Either keep them in a refrigerator, covered with clingfilm, or covered in foil in a light larder. You can buy packets of square-shaped ham slices from most supermarkets. Do not buy the extra-thin slices as they will fall apart.

20 square slices of ham
*625 g	1½ lb Brie*
cocktail sticks

Cut the Brie into 2.5cm × 15mm/1 × ½″ slices. Diagonally cut each slice of ham into 4, to give triangle shapes. Place a slice of Brie on each triangle and roll up, then spear with a cocktail stick and arrange on a serving plate. Cover and chill until ready to serve.

MAKES 80 / 🖐

Marinated Herrings and Pears with Soured Cream

A very good friend served me this unusual but delicious combination as a starter, adapted here to make cocktail canapés. Tinned pears keep their colour and moisture but really ripe, juicy fresh pears could be used instead.

1 × 350 g jar of sweet herrings in dill, drained
1 × 411 g tin of pear halves, drained
*150 ml	5 fl oz soured cream*
cocktail sticks

Cut the herring fillets and pears into small chunks. Place one of each on a cocktail stick and arrange on a serving plate around a central ramekin filled with soured cream. Chill until ready to serve.

MAKES 40 / 🖐

Stuffed Mushrooms

These are particularly good for vegetarians but also add variety to mixed canapés. Choose small, even-sized, button mushrooms, for the sake of appearance and for ease of eating. They can be made a day in advance, if wished.

3 tbsp olive oil
1 small onion, peeled and finely chopped
1 garlic clove, peeled and crushed
*450 g	1 lb button mushrooms, wiped and stalks removed and reserved*
4 slices of bread, made into fine breadcrumbs
1 dsp chopped parsley
1 tsp mixed herbs, finely chopped
salt and freshly ground black pepper
*50 g	2 oz cheddar cheese, grated*

Put the oil in a frying pan with the onion, garlic and chopped mushroom stalks. Fry gently for 10 minutes or until the onion is soft but not brown. Add the breadcrumbs and mix lightly. Add the parsley, herbs, seasoning and cheese, mix well, then leave to cool slightly. Using a teaspoon, put the crumb mixture into the hollow of each mushroom and pat down gently. Arrange the mushrooms on a serving plate. Serve at room temperature.

MAKES 30–40 / 🖐

Cocktail Sausages with Chutney

These are very quick and easy to make and always popular. Lining the baking tray with greaseproof paper makes washing-up easier afterwards.

48 cocktail sausages
2 tbsp mango chutney, finely chopped, if necessary
cocktail sticks

Preheat the oven to 200°C/400°F/gas mark 6. Roll the sausages in the chutney and then place on a baking tray. Cook, uncovered, for 30–45 minutes or until the sausages are golden brown. Cool slightly and then spear with cocktail sticks and arrange on a plate. Serve warm.

MAKES 48 / 🖐

Smoked Salmon with Avocado

This is not the most visually attractive canapé but it has a lovely natural flavour and is very popular. It is fairly quick to make but should be done within two or three hours of serving, otherwise the avocado is liable to turn brown. Not all pieces of avocado will be the correct size, so use up odd pieces in a salad.

2 ripe avocados
juice of 1 lemon
225 g / 8 oz smoked salmon, thinly sliced
freshly ground black pepper
cocktail sticks
watercress, to garnish

Cut the avocados in half and remove the stones. Cut the flesh lengthways into 5 and crossways into 6, cutting through the skin. Using a dessertspoon, scoop the flesh into a bowl and mix the chunks with the lemon juice and pepper. Cut the smoked salmon into 6 cm × 15 mm / 2½″ × ½″ strips. Spear an avocado chunk with a cocktail stick (thus keeping your hands cleaner) and place on a strip of smoked salmon. Roll up and spear with a cocktail stick. Continue until all the ingredients are used up, arranging the canapés on a serving plate. Chill and serve garnished with the watercress.

MAKES APPROX 45 / 🕯

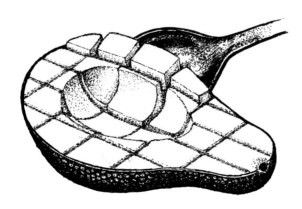

HOW TO CUT THE AVOCADO

Various Vol-au-Vents

These have a slightly 'naff' image, but with a good filling they always go down well with hungry guests. Don't bother making your own pastry cases, as bought cases are very good. They can be filled in advance and just warmed through in a low oven. Allow two per person and for a party of 20 people or more, it is worth cooking two fillings for variety.

1 packet of 60 frozen cocktail vol-au-vent cases
a little oil
1 egg
*300 ml	10 fl oz milk*
*50 g	2 oz butter*
*50 g	2 oz flour*
salt and freshly ground black pepper

Preheat the oven to 200°C/400°F/gas mark 6. Put the vol-au-vent cases on a lightly oiled baking tray with the ring-shaped cut upwards. Break the egg into a cup and add 1 dsp milk. Mix well, then brush the tops of the vol-au-vent cases with the mixture. Place in the oven and bake for about 15 minutes or until puffed and golden brown. Remove lids and leave to cool. Melt the butter in a saucepan and stir in the flour with a wooden spoon. Gradually add the milk, stirring with a wooden spoon or hand whisk to make a smooth sauce. Season to taste.

Add any of the following to the white sauce:

*225 g	8 oz chopped, cooked spinach, drained well*
freshly grated nutmeg

OR

*225 g	8 oz peeled, cooked prawns*
a dash of Tabasco
*25 g	1 oz cheddar cheese, grated*
1 sprig of parsley, chopped
a little white wine (can be used to substitute a little of the milk)

OR

*125 g	4 oz cooked chicken meat, finely chopped*
2 tbsp sweetcorn (tinned, or frozen and thawed)
1 tsp Worcestershire sauce
1 tbsp red pepper, finely chopped (optional)

OR

125 g | 4 oz button mushrooms, finely chopped and fried in a little oil
a dash of Tabasco
1 tsp Worcestershire sauce
1 sprig of fresh thyme, finely chopped

MAKES 60 VOL-AU-VENTS / ♠

Melon, Mango and Cheeses

These are pleasing mixtures of fruit and cheeses on sticks, but you can experiment with other combinations, perhaps using up bits of cheese lurking in the refrigerator and fruit from the fruit bowl. Remember the cocktail sticks.

1 ripe mango, peeled and cut into bite-sized pieces
450 g | 1 lb cheddar cheese, cut into bite-sized pieces

OR

225 g | 8 oz seedless grapes, stalks removed
450 g | 1 lb Cambozola, cut into bite-sized pieces

OR

½ small melon, skinned and cut into bite-sized pieces
450 g | 1 lb firm Brie, cut into bite-sized pieces

MAKES APPROX 60 / ♠

Fried Breakfast Kebabs

Fried breakfasts are delicious but naughty. This is the perfect answer: all the flavour but less quantity. Serve these popular canapés with a small dish of tomato ketchup mixed with a little mustard, if wished.

15 cocktail sausages
10 rashers of streaky bacon, rind removed
175 g | 6 oz button mushrooms, wiped, stalks removed and halved crossways
175 g | 6 oz cherry tomatoes, halved
cocktail sticks
a little oil

Cut each sausage into 4 slices. Cut the rashers in half lengthways, then each half into 3 strips. Roll up tightly. Thread a piece of sausage, mushroom half, bacon roll and tomato half onto a cocktail stick then place on a grill pan. Repeat until all the ingredients are used. Heat grill to high, brush the kebabs with a little oil and cook for about 3 minutes, then turn and repeat until the sausage and bacon are brown and crisp. Arrange on a serving plate and keep warm until ready to serve with the sauce.

MAKES 60 / 🍾🍾

Turkey-Stuffing Meatballs with Cranberry Dip

I love Christmas turkey stuffing but I only taste it once a year, so I devised these as year-round treats. If you cannot buy sausage-meat, buy sausages and remove their skins. Rolling the mixture is very messy and I only hope your phone does not ring!

1 small onion, peeled and finely chopped
1 stick of celery, strings removed and very finely chopped
a little oil
225 g | 8 oz sausage-meat
1 × 400 g | 14 oz tin of chestnut purée, unsweetened
salt and freshly ground black pepper
1 × 150 g | 5 oz jar of cranberry sauce
cocktail sticks

Put the onion, celery and oil in a frying pan and cook gently for about 5 minutes or until soft. Put the sausage-meat and chestnut purée in a bowl and mix well by hand. Add the onion mixture, season and mix again. Preheat the oven to 200°C/400°F/gas mark 6. Take a teaspoonful, roll into a ball in the palm of your hand, then place on an oiled baking tray. Repeat until the mixture is used up. Bake in the oven for about 20 minutes or until the balls are slightly brown and sizzling. Remove and arrange on a warm serving plate with a pot of cranberry sauce in the middle.

MAKES 30 / ♦♦ / FREEZE

Barbecued Meatballs

Make these in the same way as the turkey-stuffing meatballs. Serve with a tomato relish dip in a ramekin, if wished.

1 small onion, peeled and finely chopped
a little oil
1 tsp mixed chopped herbs, fresh or dried
225 g / 8 oz lean mince, finely ground
1 egg
50 g / 2 oz fine breadcrumbs
a dash of Worcestershire sauce
a dash of Tabasco sauce
1 tsp mustard
salt and freshly ground black pepper
cocktail sticks

MAKES 30 / ♦ / FREEZE

Roll-Up Bacon Ideas

These canapés can all be made in advance and warmed through at the last minute after they have been arranged on a serving plate. Remember the cocktail sticks.

15 rashers back bacon, rind removed, cut in half lengthways then across to make 4 strips
450 g / 1 lb chicken livers
a knob of butter
1 tsp mixed herbs
1 garlic clove, peeled and crushed (optional)

Cook the livers in the butter and herbs until brown on the outside but slightly pink inside. Leave to cool, then cut up livers to appropriate bite-sized pieces.

OR

1 × 400 g / 14 oz tin of prunes, halved and stones removed

OR

5 bananas, skinned and cut into bite-sized pieces

Preheat the oven to 200°C/400°F/gas mark 6. Roll the bacon round any of these fillings and secure with a cocktail stick. Place on a baking tray, and cook for 15 minutes or until the bacon is done. Serve hot.

MAKES APPROX 60 / 🍸🍸 / FREEZE WITH LIVERS/PRUNES ONLY

Smoked Salmon Whirls

These are very simple to make and can be kept in the freezer until you are ready to cut them up. You could substitute cream cheese mixed with chopped chives for the butter.

8 slices of brown bread, thin cut
a little butter, softened
225 g / 8 oz of smoked salmon, thinly sliced
freshly ground black pepper
lemon juice

Using a rolling pin, thinly roll out each slice of bread. Spread each slice with butter and overlap to join 2 slices together to get a longer roll. Lay the smoked salmon on top, season with pepper and sprinkle with lemon juice. Roll up tightly, holding the shorter side, and wrap each in clingfilm. Chill. Cut into 15 mm / ½″ slices and arrange on a plate.

MAKES APPROX 40 / 🍾🍾 / FREEZE

Cheese Straws

These are quick and easy to make and can be stored in an airtight jar until needed. Mustard is added to enhance the flavour of the cheese. Sprinkle a little extra grated cheese over the straws before cooking if you want them to look more rugged.

125 g / 4 oz plain flour
salt and cayenne pepper
50 g / 2 oz butter
50 g / 2 oz cheddar cheese, or Red Leicester for colour, grated
1 tsp whole-grain mustard
1 egg yolk

Preheat the oven to 200°C/400°F/gas mark 6. Put the flour, salt and pepper in a bowl. Cut in the butter and rub in the flour with your fingertips until the mixture resembles fine breadcrumbs. Using a round-bladed knife, stir in the grated cheese, mustard, egg yolk and then gradually add 2 tbsp cold water until a stiff dough forms. Knead lightly on a floured surface. Roll out 15mm/½″ thick and cut into 6 mm × 5 cm / ¼″ × 2″ strips. Put on a greased baking tray, twisting the strips if you like, and bake for about 15 minutes or until golden brown. Cool on a wire rack.

MAKES APPROX 20 / 🍾🍾

Blueberry Muffins with Smoked Mackerel Mousse

This might sound a bit strange, but whenever I have persuaded our clients to try it, it has always become a favourite. If you can't get fresh, tinned or frozen blueberries, use blackcurrants or buy one packet of blueberry muffin mix and don't tell anyone! If you do not have tartlet tins, buy baby petit four paper cups and remove the cases after cooking.

*175 g	6 oz butter*
*225 g	8 oz caster sugar*
3 large eggs
a few drops of vanilla essence
*225 g	8 oz self-raising flour*
*4 tbsp blueberries, or 1 × 215 g	7½ oz tin of blackcurrants, drained*
*225 g	8 oz smoked mackerel fillets, skinned*
*125 g	4 oz cream cheese*
freshly ground black pepper
juice of ½ lemon
a little cream

Preheat the oven to 190°C/375°F/gas mark 5. Put the butter, sugar, eggs, vanilla essence and flour in a bowl and beat until well blended and smooth. Fold in the blueberries or blackcurrants and, using a teaspoon, put the mixture into petit four cups or buttered and floured tartlet tins. Bake for about 15 minutes or until the sponge is risen, slightly brown and just cooked. Remove from the tins or cups and cool. Blend the mackerel, cream cheese and pepper in a blender until smooth and add a little cream to soften to a smooth piping consistency. Put into a piping bag and pipe a whirl on top of each muffin. Chill until ready to serve. Garnish with extra blueberries if you wish.

MAKES APPROX 60 / ♦♦ / FREEZE MUFFINS ONLY

Choux Balls with Stilton and Port

These are a great favourite, especially with men, as they are a good mouthful, with a hint of alcohol. The choux balls can be made in advance and frozen.

75 g | 3 oz plain flour
a pinch of salt
150 ml | 5 fl oz half water and half milk
50 g | 2 oz butter
2 large eggs
125 g | 4 oz Stilton, crumbled
125 g | 4 oz cream cheese
a little cream
a splash of port
25 g | 1 oz walnuts, finely chopped

Preheat the oven to 200°C/400°F/gas mark 6. Sift the flour and salt into a bowl. Put the water and milk into a saucepan with the butter and bring slowly to the boil, making sure that the butter melts. Remove from the heat, quickly tip in the flour and beat until the mixture leaves the side of the pan clean and has a sheen. Beat in the eggs gradually to make a smooth paste. Using two teaspoons, spoon walnut-sized pieces onto a greased baking tray about 5 cm / 2″ apart, allowing for expansion. Bake for about 15 minutes or until golden brown and crisp.

Remove, cool slightly and then cut three quarters of the way through each one. Put the Stilton, cream cheese, cream, port and walnuts into a bowl and mash with a fork until creamy but still holding shape. Using a teaspoon, spoon some in each choux ball, close up, pile on a serving plate and serve chilled.

MAKES 25–30 / ♥♥ / FREEZE CHOUX BALLS ONLY

Quail Eggs with Bacon

This is a novel cocktail canapé and a good talking point. Make sure the bacon is only just cooked, because if it is too crispy the eggs won't stay in place. Choose back or streaky depending on how much fat you like. Serve at room temperature and, for convenience, you can make them a few hours in advance.

oil for shallow frying
4 slices of white bread, medium cut
4 rashers of back bacon, rind removed
36 quail eggs
freshly ground black pepper

Heat the oil in a frying pan until hot but not smoking. Add the bread, a slice at a time, and fry, turning once until golden brown on each side. Drain on kitchen roll. Cut each slice into 3 and then across in 3 to give 9 squares. Pour off most of the oil and gently fry the bacon, until just cooked. Drain, then leave to cool on kitchen roll. Lower the temperature of the oil, then fry the eggs, about 6 at a time, until the white is firm but the yolk is still runny. Remove carefully with a spatula and place on a flat surface. Repeat until all the eggs are cooked. Trim off any straggling edges of white with a sharp knife or scissors. Cut the bacon into squares to fit the fried bread and place one on each fried bread square. Place a fried egg on top, then arrange on a serving place. Garnish them with freshly ground black pepper.

MAKES 36 / 👭

Scrambled Egg and Anchovy Toasties

If you like your scrambled egg well cooked (like rubber!) then forget this recipe – your egg would come bouncing off the toast. The toasties can be made one or two hours in advance.

8 slices of white bread, medium cut
oil for shallow frying
4 eggs
2 tbsp milk
50 g / 2 oz butter
salt and freshly ground black pepper
1 × 50 g / 2 oz tin of anchovy fillets, drained

Thinly cut the crusts off the bread. Heat the oil until hot but not smoking and fry the bread on both sides until golden brown. Drain on kitchen roll. Cut each slice diagonally

Paw Paw, Avocado and Grapefruit (page 46) with Corn Bread (page 151).

Left: Peking Duck (page 37); right, clockwise from top: Blueberry Muffins with Smoked Mackerel Mousse (page 30), Ham Round Brie (page 19), Scrambled Egg and Anchovy Toasties (page 32), Tomato, Mozzarella and Black Olive Kebabs (page 25); bottom: Smoked Mussel Dip (page 18) with crudités.

Paw Paw and Ricotta (page 49) with Delphi Lodge Bread (page 152).

Avocado, Scallop and Bacon Salad (page 52).

Quail Egg Nests (page 53).

Trout with Mustard Sauce (page 64).

Salmon Steaks with Honey and Ginger (page 67).

into 4 and then each triangle in half again to make 8 triangles. Put the eggs, milk and butter in a small saucepan and, using a wooden spoon, stir over a low heat a few seconds until the eggs are creamy and just scrambled. Remember to stop stirring over the heat before the egg is done, as it goes on cooking in the saucepan. Season with very little salt, since the anchovies are salty, and lots of pepper. Using a teaspoon, spoon a little egg onto each triangle of fried bread, then cut each anchovy fillet into 4–5 pieces and place a piece on top of the egg. Arrange on a serving plate and serve at room temperature.

MAKES 60 / 👣

Smoked Salmon and Spinach Roulade

You can make these fresh and attractive-looking canapés a day in advance, then cut them up at the last minute.

*300 g	10 oz packet of frozen spinach, defrosted and roughly chopped*
5 eggs, separated
a little freshly grated nutmeg
salt and freshly ground black pepper
*225 g	8 oz cream cheese*
3–5 tbsp milk
*225 g	8 oz smoked salmon, thinly sliced*

Preheat the oven to 190°C/375°F/gas mark 5. Line a 20 cm × 30 cm / 8″ × 12″ baking tray with greaseproof paper. Put the spinach and egg yolks in a bowl, season and mix well. Whisk the egg whites until stiff, then fold into the spinach mixture. Pour into the lined baking tray and bake for 10 minutes or until set but not brown. Remove from the oven and leave to cool. Turn the cooked spinach and egg mixture over and out onto another piece of greaseproof paper. Spread to the edges with the cream cheese, thinned with enough milk to make it spreadable. Season with pepper, then lay the smoked salmon on top, making sure the salmon reaches to the edges. Cut the roulade in half lengthways, then tightly roll up each piece, holding the longer edges. Wrap in clingfilm to keep it rolled. Refrigerate until ready to serve. Cut crossways into 6 mm / ¼″ slices and arrange on a serving plate.

MAKES 40 👣

Yorkshire Puds with Rare Roast Beef or Toad-in-the-Hole

These tiny canapés are tasty and a good talking point because of their size, but you do need pastry case tins with 4 cm | 1½" diameter cups. Both can be cooked in advance and frozen for up to one month. Just thaw and warm through before serving. Freeze the Yorkshire Puds without their beef topping.

For the batter:
*125 g	4 oz self-raising flour*
a pinch of salt
2 eggs
*300 ml	10 fl oz half milk and half water*
a little oil

For the Yorkshire Puds:
*175 g	6 oz thinly sliced, rare roast beef*
1 tbsp horseradish sauce

For Toad-in-the-Hole:
12 cooked cocktail sausages
1 tbsp tomato ketchup

Preheat the oven to 220°C/425°F/gas mark 7. Put the flour and salt in a bowl or blender. Add the eggs and milk and mix with a hand-held electric whisk, or in a blender, until smooth, thick and fluffy. Transfer to a pouring jug. Put a few drops of oil in each baking tin, then fill half-way up with batter mixture. Bake for about 10 minutes or until the batter is well risen and brown. For Toad-in-the-Hole, cut each cocktail sausage into 5 pieces and place a slice in each batter-filled cup before cooking. When cool, top with a little tomato ketchup and serve. For the Yorkshire Puds, cut the beef slices into 2.5 cm / 1" squares, scrunch up and place on top of each pudding, then spoon a little horseradish on top, according to taste.

MAKES 60 / ♣♣ / FREEZE (EXCEPT BEEF)

Blinis with Smoked Salmon and Soured Cream

The blinis are a real pain to make but if you get down to it on a dark, rainy winter's day, then freeze them, it can be very satisfying and therapeutic. All the ingredients should be hand warm to get the best from the yeast. If you want you can make some additional, larger blinis for a starter.

1 tsp dried yeast
*175 g	6 oz plain flour*
*25g	1 oz salted butter, melted*
1 egg, separated
1 heaped tsp caster sugar
*150 ml	5 fl oz hand-warm milk*
oil for frying
*250 g	9 oz smoked salmon, thinly cut*
*150 ml	5 fl oz soured cream*
*1 × 200 g	7 oz jar of Danish lumpfish roe*
1 lemon, to garnish

Pour 150 ml / 5 fl oz warm water into a jug and sprinkle over the yeast. Whisk, then leave for 10 minutes to froth. Put half the flour into a bowl and pour in the yeast mixture. Beat well with a whisk, cover with a cloth and leave in a warm place for about 30 minutes, *or* until it is well risen. Slowly add the rest of the flour then the melted butter, egg yolk and caster sugar. Beat the mixture well with a wooden spoon, then add the warm milk and whisk again. Cover and leave to rise again in a warm place for 30–60 minutes. Whisk the egg white in a small bowl and then fold into the batter. Cover and leave to rise again for 1 hour.

Heat a little oil in a large, flat, non-stick frying pan, wipe round with kitchen roll and then, using a teaspoon, pour in little blobs of batter and let each blini spread out, thicker than pancakes. Cook until slightly brown, about 30 seconds, then turn over with a spatula and cook for a further few seconds to brown. Pile up on a plate. To finish the blinis, place a spoonful of soured cream and a scrunch of smoked salmon on each baby blini and then top with a little Danish 'caviar'. Arrange on a serving plate and garnish with lemon wedges. Napkins need to be at hand!

MAKES APPROX 60 / ♨♨♨ / FREEZE BLINIS ONLY

Baby Hamburgers

Prime Minister John Major inspired this idea. One day when I was cooking for him he jokingly asked for a hamburger from a well-known chain, so I went and bought him one. The next time I did the catering at a cocktail party for him I concocted these; Norma Major recognised the joke immediately. In all seriousness, they are delicious and have become a great party favourite.

For the baps:
1 tsp yeast
150 ml / 5 fl oz half milk and half water
225 g / 8 oz plain flour
salt
25 g / 1 oz lard
25 g / 1 oz sesame seeds

For the hamburgers and filling:
350 g / 12 oz lean minced beef
1 dsp Worcestershire sauce
1 small onion, peeled and grated
1 tsp mixed herbs
salt and freshly ground black pepper
1 egg
5 slices processed cheese
1 box of cherry tomatoes, or 1 tbsp tomato relish
cocktail sticks

Mix the yeast with the lukewarm milk and water and stir until dissolved. Put the flour and 2 pinches of salt in a bowl and rub in the lard with your fingertips. Stir in the liquid and work the dough until firm. Place on a floured surface and knead for 3 minutes. Put in a bowl, cover with a cloth and leave for 2 hours in a warm place to rise. Preheat the oven to 190°C/375°F/gas mark 5. Knead the dough again on the floured surface and then roll a little mixture, the size of a small marble, in the palm of your hands. Slightly flatten and then place on a greased baking tray. Brush with a little milk and then put a few sesame seeds on each bap top. Repeat until all the dough is used. Bake for about 15 minutes or until the baps are lightly brown.

To make the hamburgers, put the mince, Worcestershire sauce, grated onion, herbs, salt, pepper and the egg in a bowl and mix well with your hand. Roll into small, marble-sized balls and flatten a little. Place on a greased baking tray and when all the mixture is used bake 10 minutes or until each hamburger is just cooked. Meanwhile, cut each slice of processed cheese into 16 squares (4 by 4) and thinly slice the cherry tomatoes. Cut each bap in half, inset a hamburger, top with a square of cheese and finally a slice of tomato or the tomato relish. Replace the top of the bap and secure with a cocktail stick. Repeat until all the baps are used and arrange on a serving place. Serve at room temperature or slightly warmed.

MAKES APPROX 80 / ♠♠♠ / FREEZE BUNS AND BURGERS SEPARATELY

Peking Duck

This without doubt is one of our all-time favourites at cocktail parties. It takes time to make but the pancakes can be made in advance and frozen. The duck, however, should be cooked on the day to keep its crispy texture. Some supermarkets sell ready-made pancakes.

1 × 3 kilo / 7 lb duck
18 pancakes (see page 54)
½ × 450 g / 1 lb jar plum sauce
1 large cucumber, cut into 2.5 cm / 1″ strips
2 bunches of spring onions, cut into 2.5 cm / 1″ strips
cocktail sticks

Preheat the oven to 200°C/400°F/gas mark 6. Cook the duck for 1 ½ hours, or until very crisp. Cool, then shred the duck flesh and place in a bowl. Cut each pancake into 4 × 5 cm / 2″ strips. Lay them out, brush generously with the plum sauce, then place the duck flesh on top, followed by cucumber and spring onion strips. Roll up, spear with a cocktail stick, arrange on a serving plate, then serve.

MAKES 70 / ♠♠♠

Dinner Parties

Spare time seems to come in spates these days, so it is important to use the breaks for organising the busier times. Dinner parties are dwindling because people are so busy, but using recipes that can be prepared in advance and tucked under the lid of a freezer makes entertaining that much less stressful. Here are many quick, simple meals that are also delicious and look smart to boot, such as Avocado with Strawberry Purée (see page 44), George Butler III Steaks (see page 78) and then Flaming Crème Caramels (see page 111). This would all take very little time and you would have no complaints, sending away many happy people. It's a tough old world and we all need to treat our friends now and again, so stop talking about those dinner parties that you are always going to have 'tomorrow', and start cooking! Listed here are some balanced menus, ranging from quick and easy to challenging and time-consuming. Once you get used to the book, you can sort out your own menus.

After the main courses, I give a few special recipes for vegetables to accompany them, but do also remember the more 'ordinary' ones such as broccoli or courgettes – with lots of butter!

Suggested Dinner-Party Menus

Quick and Easy

FRESH SALMON PÂTÉ	AVOCADO WITH STRAWBERRY PURÉE
SWEET AND SOUR CHICKEN	TROUT WITH MUSTARD SAUCE
BELGIAN WAFFLES WITH ADVOCAAT	EXCRUCIATING CHOCOLATE PUDDING
•••	•••
PARMA HAM WITH FRUIT	PAW PAW, AVOCADO AND GRAPEFRUIT
BARBECUED LAMB CHOPS	BOBOTIE
ICE-CREAM WITH HOT CHERRIES	FLAMBÉED BANANAS

Harder and More Time-Consuming

DUCK EGGS AND SOLDIERS	WINSLOW STUFFED MUSHROOMS
CHICKEN DIVAN	SALMON STEAKS WITH BACON AND ROSEMARY
LEMON MOUSSE	STRAWBERRIES WITH ZABAGLIONE
•••	•••
QUAIL EGG NESTS	AVOCADO, SCALLOP AND BACON SALAD
BASS WITH TOMATO AND BASIL SAUCE	STUFFED LEG OF LAMB
TIRAMISU	KINKY PIE

Definitely Challenging and Time-Consuming

SMOKED SALMON WITH SCRAMBLED EGG	FILO PIZZAS
SCALLOPS IN PASTRY SHELLS	SPECIAL FISH PIE
BEIGNETS WITH LEMON SAUCE	GRAND MARNIER SOUFFLÉS
•••	•••
JERUSALEM ARTICHOKE MOUSSES WITH BACON	SCALLOP MOUSSES WITH ASPARAGUS SAUCE
HARE IN CHOCOLATE SAUCE	CARIBBEAN LAMB PARCELS
LEMON OR LIME MERINGUE PIE	FLOATING ISLANDS

Carrot-Top Soup

Most people throw away carrot tops or give them to their pet rabbits. But carrot-top soup is, in fact, delicious. It can be served hot or chilled so wait and see what the weather is like.

1 onion, peeled and chopped
a little oil
*225 g	8 oz potatoes, peeled and chopped*
1 bunch of carrot tops, washed very well, the tougher stalks removed
*600 ml	1 pt milk*
*300 ml	10 fl oz Chicken Stock (see page 155)*
salt and freshly ground black pepper

Fry the onion in the oil for a few minutes to soften, then add the potatoes and carrot tops. Stir, then add rest of the ingredients. Cover and simmer for 30 minutes or until the potatoes are cooked. Put into a blender and blend until smooth, then serve hot or chilled.

SERVES 6–8 / 🌶🌶 / FREEZE

French Onion Soup with Brandy

This great soup is glamorised by the floating Gruyère-topped toast. It is also very good for keeping winter colds at bay.

*450 g	1 lb onions, peeled, sliced thinly and roughly chopped*
1 garlic clove, peeled and crushed
*50 g	2 oz butter*
*25 g	1 oz flour*
*1.2 litres	2 pints Chicken Stock (see page 155)*
salt and freshly ground black pepper
*6 slices of French bread, 15 mm	½" thick*
125 g |4 oz Gruyère cheese, grated
4 tbsp brandy, or more

Put the onions, garlic and butter in a large, heavy-based saucepan and cook for 10 minutes or until the onion is soft and slightly brown. Mix in the flour, then stir in the stock and season. Cook, covered, over a low heat for 30 minutes. Meanwhile, grill the bread on one side until light brown. Turn over, top with the Gruyère cheese, then grill again until the cheese is bubbling. Add the brandy to the soup, place a toast in each bowl, then pour over the soup. The toast will float to the top. Serve hot.

SERVES 6 / 🌶🌶

Gazpacho

This is very easy to make, with no cooking involved except frying the bread. It is perfect on a summer's day and very healthy as well. The garnishes are fun but not essential, if you are short of time.

6 ripe tomatoes

1 garlic clove, peeled

½ onion, peeled and roughly chopped

½ cucumber, peeled and roughly chopped

1 red pepper, cored, deseeded and chunked

a sprig of thyme

a sprig of basil

4 sprigs of parsley

4 tbsp olive oil

juice of 1 lemon

1 tsp sugar

salt and freshly ground black pepper

a dash of Tabasco

1 × 450 ml | 16 fl oz jar tomato juice

For the garnish:

¼ cucumber, peeled and finely chopped

1 small red pepper, cored, deseeded and finely chopped

4 slices of bread, crusts removed and cut into 15 mm | ½" cubes

1 garlic clove, peeled and crushed

4 tbsp olive oil

Using a sharp knife, nick each tomato skin. Boil a saucepan of water and lower in the tomatoes. Leave for 30 seconds or until the cut in the skin starts to split. Drain immediately and run under cold water for 1 minute. Peel the skins and discard. Put all the ingredients, including the tomatoes, in a large bowl and mix. Using an electric blender, blend the ingredients in 2 or 3 lots, depending on the size of the machine, and pour into a soup tureen. Taste for seasoning and chill until ready to serve. Meanwhile, shallow fry the bread cubes in the olive oil and crushed garlic until golden brown. Drain on kitchen roll. Serve with the garnishes passed round separately in bowls.

SERVES 6 / ❧

Vichyssoise

This soup has many versions but, after a great deal of experimenting, this is my favourite. For vegetarians, omit the stock and use extra milk instead. Many people automatically discard the tops of leeks, but you can use all but very tough, dark-green leaves in this recipe.

a little oil
1 medium-sized onion, peeled and chopped
3 medium-sized leeks, chopped and washed
3 medium-sized potatoes, peeled and chopped
1 bunch of watercress
*600 ml	1 pint milk*
*450 ml	15 fl oz chicken stock*
salt and freshly ground black pepper
*150 ml	5 fl oz double cream*
freshly ground nutmeg

Put the oil in a large, heavy-based saucepan, then add the onion and leeks. Fry gently without colouring for about 5 minutes. Add the potatoes, watercress, milk, stock and seasoning. Bring to the boil, then reduce to a low simmer, cover and cook for about 20 minutes or until the potatoes are cooked. Cool, then blend in a blender or pass through a fine sieve. Add the cream and chill. Pour into soup bowls, then garnish with the freshly ground nutmeg.

SERVES 4–6 / 🍶

Avocado with Strawberry Purée

This is the perfect starter for the amateur cook or anyone short of time. Delicious, fresh and colourful, just serve it with warm Corn Bread (see page 151).

*300 g	10 oz strawberries, washed and hulled*
4 tbsp French Dressing (see page 153)
1 tsp caster sugar (optional)
4 ripe avocados
freshly ground black pepper
lemon wedges

Purée the strawberries with the French Dressing and add the sugar if the strawberries are not sweet enough. Cut the avocados in half lengthways and remove the stones. Carefully peel off the skins. Just before serving, whisk the purée again and pour enough to cover the bottom of each plate. Either place each avocado half, cut-side down, onto the purée or slice the flesh lengthways and fan the slices onto the purée. Season with fresh pepper and garnish with lemon wedges.

SERVES 8 / 🌶

Parma Ham with Fruit

This foolproof, delicious, fresh starter or low-calorie lunch can be arranged on the plates in advance, but cover them with a damp cloth to prevent the Parma ham drying at the edges. Melon is usually served with Parma ham, but here are a few other suggestions. Serve with warm bread.

12 slices of Parma ham

1 ripe Ogen melon, quartered, pips removed, then each quarter cut lengthways into 3 slices and skinned

OR

12 ripe figs, skinned, then carefully cut into quarters, attached at the base, and each quarter halved, to make 8 'petals'. Open up and this will make a flower shape

OR

1 ripe mango, peeled and sliced from the stone

freshly ground black pepper

Place two slices of Parma ham on each plate and decorate with the chosen fruit. Grind over some pepper and serve.

SERVES 6 / 🌶

Paw Paw, Avocado and Grapefruit

Simple, colourful and healthy. The ingredients must be perfect, otherwise it is not worth doing – buy in advance to make sure.

1 ripe paw paw
2 ripe avocados
juice of ½ lemon
1 pink grapefruit
salt and freshly ground black pepper
6 tsp hazelnut or walnut oil

Cut the paw paw in half and discard the pips. Using a sharp knife, remove the skin, cut each half into 4–5 slices lengthways and set aside. Cut the avocados in half and discard the stone. Peel, then slice each half lengthways into 4–5 slices, and coat with lemon juice. Using a sharp knife, peel the grapefruits as you would an apple, removing the skin and pith, then cut in between each segment to release the flesh. Discard or drink the juice. Arrange the slices on individual plates, sprinkle with salt and pepper and then drizzle over the oil.

SERVES 6 🖐

Fresh Salmon Pâté

This quick, easy lunch snack or smart dinner party starter is even faster to prepare if you cook the salmon in a microwave for two minutes on medium heat or until cooked. Serve with piping-hot toast.

225 g | 8 oz fresh salmon, filleted
1 tbsp Mayonnaise (see page 154)
2 tbsp soured cream
juice of ½ lemon
5 cm | 2" cucumber, peeled and finely chopped
freshly ground black pepper
a few leaves of fresh basil, chopped (optional)

Poach the salmon in a covered saucepan with a little water or white wine for about 10 minutes or until cooked. Leave to cool, then peel and discard the skin, plus any juice. Put the salmon into a bowl with the rest of the ingredients and mix gently with a fork, to keep the flaky texture. Transfer to a pâté dish and chill until ready to serve.

SERVES 4 / 🖐

Chicken-Liver Pâté

My godmother, an excellent cook, has been making this pâté for years. It is very rich and best left refrigerated for about three days to allow the brandy and port to mellow under the butter lid. When you cut through the top, the aroma is wonderful. Serve with piping hot toast.

*50 g	2 oz butter*
2 garlic cloves, peeled and crushed
*450 g	1 lb chicken livers*
a splash of brandy
a splash of port
salt and freshly ground black pepper
1 tsp chopped thyme, fresh or dried
For the topping:
*125 g	4 oz butter*
1 tsp dried oregano
2 bay leaves

Melt the butter in a large frying pan and add the garlic and chicken livers. Cook over a low heat for about 5 minutes, stirring occasionally, until the chicken livers are brown outside but still pink inside. Add the brandy, port, seasoning and thyme and stir well. Put into a blender, blend until smooth, then pour into a pâté dish. Smooth over the top. Melt the remaining butter in a small saucepan with the oregano, then pour over the pâté. Garnish with the bay leaves. Chill until ready to serve.

SERVES 8–10 / ♦

Kipper Pâté with Whisky

This is quick and easy, and you can keep a supply of frozen kippers in the freezer ready for an emergency. The breadcrumbs prevent the kippers tasting too strong and the whisky blends in well. Serve with hot brown toast.

225 g / 8 oz kipper fillets, defrosted if frozen
175 g / 6 oz butter, melted
juice of 1 small lemon
150 ml / 5 fl oz soured cream
125 g / 4 oz fine breadcrumbs, brown or white
freshly ground black pepper
1 tbsp whisky
parsley sprigs

Put all the ingredients except the parsley in a blender and blend until smooth. Transfer to a pâté dish and chill. Garnish with parsley before serving.

SERVES 6–8 / 🍶

Goat-Cheese Salad

Simple and yet one of the smartest starters, this is also good for a supper or lunch main course. Use up salad leaves from the refrigerator, your own, home-grown favourites, or a ready-mixed bag.

6 handfuls of salad leaves such as curly endive, Cos lettuce, rocket, lamb's tongues, oakleaf, radicchio, watercress or round lettuce
2 fresh goat-cheese logs, approx 20 cm × 6 cm / 8″ × 2½″
6 dsp hazelnut, walnut or Virgin olive oil
salt and freshly ground black pepper

Preheat the oven to 200°C/400°F/gas mark 6. Divide the washed and prepared salad onto 6 small plates. Slice the goat-cheese logs into 6 slices each and place on a flat baking tray. Bake for 5 minutes or until the cheese is soft. Remove from the oven and transfer 2 slices to each plate, on top of the salad. Dribble over the oil, then season with salt and pepper. Serve immediately.

SERVES 6 / 🍶

Smoked Salmon with Smoked Mackerel Mousse

This very popular starter can also be served, as smaller parcels, at a cocktail party. As an extra touch, cut tiny strands of cucumber skin and wrap them like string round each parcel, or serve with marinated cucumber slices (see Cucumber and Strawberry Salad, page 146).

2 smoked mackerel fillets, skinned
225 g / 8 oz cream cheese
freshly ground black pepper
a dash of Tabasco
a little milk
1 dsp chopped chives (optional)
225 g / 8 oz smoked salmon, thinly sliced
4 lemon wedges
4 dill sprigs

Put the mackerel, cream cheese, pepper and Tabasco in a blender and blend until smooth. Add a little milk to thin the mixture but it should hold its shape. Stir in the chives if using. Cut the smoked salmon into 8 strips about 2.5 cm × 10 cm / 1″ × 4″. Spoon some smoked mackerel mixture onto each strip and roll up or make into a parcel. Chill, then garnish each plate with a lemon wedge and dill.

SERVES 4 / ●

Paw Paw and Ricotta

Not only is this an unusual and very easy starter but also a perfect snack lunch, slimming and healthy. Serve with Corn Bread (see page 151).

1 ripe paw paw
50 g / 2 oz Ricotta
a little olive oil
salt and freshly ground black pepper

Cut the paw paw in half lengthways, like an avocado, scoop out the black pips with a dessertspoon, then discard. Crumble the Ricotta into the middle of each paw paw half, drizzle over a little olive oil and season well.

SERVES 2 / ●

Ravioli Starter

Good, fresh ravioli with delicious fillings such as Gorgonzola with walnut or smoked salmon with Mascarpone is now available from supermarkets and Italian specialty shops, with pasta machines churning out all shapes and sizes. Ravioli make a quick, easy starter or a main course for busy people or those who don't like to spend a lot of time cooking.

20 ravioli parcels (32 for main course)
4 dsp virgin olive oil
a few leaves of fresh sage, basil or oregano per person, finely chopped
salt and freshly ground black pepper
4 tomatoes, sliced

Boil a generous amount of salted water and, when bubbling, carefully lower in the ravioli. Fresh pasta takes about 3 minutes; follow packet instructions for dried. Drain in a colander. Pour a dessertspoon of virgin olive oil per person in the saucepan, add the chopped sage, basil or oregano and return the ravioli. Toss gently to coat each parcel with oil, transfer to plates, then garnish with pepper and sliced tomato.

SERVES 4 / ☙

Duck Eggs and Soldiers

This amusing starter reminds me of my childhood, although not with the smoked salmon! If you can't get duck eggs, use large, free-range hen's eggs. Serve them in large egg cups or stand the eggs in napkin rings.

6 duck eggs
50 g	2 oz butter, plus extra for spreading
4 tbsp milk
salt and freshly ground black pepper
6 slices of brown bread, medium cut
125 g	4 oz smoked salmon, thinly sliced
lemon juice
Danish black lump-fish roe

Break the eggs very carefully, cutting off the top as if you were eating a boiled egg. Empty the raw eggs into a heavy-based saucepan with 50 g / 2 oz butter, milk and pepper. Wash out the shells and place in the egg cups, discarding the tops. Spread the bread with the remaining butter and place the smoked salmon on the top of each slice. Sprinkle with lemon juice and season with pepper. Remove the crusts and cut each slice into 4 lengths, or 'soldiers'. Cook the egg mixture over a very low heat, stirring continuously with a wooden spoon, until creamy and scrambled. Remove from the heat just before it is ready, as it goes on cooking in the pan. Continue stirring off the heat, then spoon into each egg shell. Place each egg cup on a plate, put 4 'soldiers' on each plate and garnish with lump-fish roe on top of the egg.

SERVES 6 / 🍶🍶

Winslow Stuffed Mushrooms

I used to have a house near Taunton, in the depths of the country. Next to us was a dairy farm and, come the autumn, the fields were white with huge, flat mushrooms. We had to invent many recipes, so we didn't waste them, but this is my favourite. It makes a very good starter for a dinner party.

4 large or medium-sized flat mushrooms
2–4 tbsp olive oil
25 g / 1 oz butter
1 onion, peeled and finely chopped
1 garlic clove, peeled and crushed
4 slices of granary bread, made into breadcrumbs
juice of 1 lemon
salt and freshly ground black pepper
1 tsp oregano, finely chopped
1 tbsp Parmesan, grated

Preheat the oven to 190°C/375°F/gas mark 5. Wipe the mushrooms, remove the stalks, then finely chop the stalks. Heat 2 tbsp oil and the butter in a frying pan, add the stalks, onion and garlic, then cook gently for 5 minutes, stirring occasionally. Add the breadcrumbs, lemon, seasoning and oregano, then stir well. Add more oil if necessary; the mixture should be quite wet. Spoon the stuffing onto the mushrooms, spreading it out to the edges and pressing down. Place the mushrooms on a greased baking tray and cover with foil. Bake for 15–20 minutes or until the mushrooms are soft and steaming. Sprinkle over the grated Parmesan and serve warm.

SERVES 4 / 🍶🍶

Seafood Pancakes

The two tricks to making perfect pancakes are to measure the batter with a serving spoon, thus ensuring that each pancake is the same size, and to wipe the frying pan with a kitchen towel soaked in oil, since pouring oil in the pan after each pancake produces too much fat. The first pancake is always the hardest as the pan has to reach the correct temperature, so try not to stop, once you start. Vary the fillings by adding different fish and herbs.

For the pancakes:

125 g | 4 oz flour

a pinch of salt

2 eggs

300 ml | 10 fl oz milk

a few sprigs of parsley

a dash of Tabasco

a little oil, for frying

For the filling:

225 g | 8 oz smoked cod or smoked haddock

300 ml | 10 fl oz milk

50 g | 2 oz butter

50 g | 2 oz flour

125 g | 4 oz prawns, cooked and shelled

125 g | 4 oz cockles and/or mussels, cooked and shelled

50 g | 2 oz cheddar cheese, grated

salt and freshly ground black pepper

a dash of Worcestershire sauce

lemon wedges

parsley

HOW TO FOLD THE PANCAKES

To make the pancakes, put all the batter ingredients in a blender and blend on high for 1 minute, making sure that the flour does not stick to the sides. Leave to stand for 15 minutes or longer. Soak kitchen towel in oil and wipe round a small, preheated frying pan. Put in 1 tablespoon of batter, spreading it out by tilting the pan. Cook on a high heat, turning until golden on both sides. Repeat until the batter is used up, making 12 or more pancakes. Pile the pancakes up and cover with a damp cloth. To make the filling, poach the cod or haddock in the milk for about 5 minutes or until cooked. Strain the milk and reserve. Flake the fish and check for bones. Melt the butter in a small saucepan, stir in the flour and then pour in the warm milk, stirring continuously, until the sauce is smooth. Add the fish, shellfish, cheese, seasoning and Worcestershire sauce. Stir well. Fold each pancake in half, in half again, then fill one pocket. Place on warm plates and let the mixture flow out onto the plate. Garnish with the lemon and parsley.

SERVES 6 / 🐚🐚 / FREEZE

Oysters Rockefeller

I spent my childhood splashing, wading and swimming over the Helford oyster beds, so oysters never seemed a treat, but later in New Orleans I discovered this dish and it completely changed my view. Give it a go and I'm sure you will understand why.

4 spring onions, peeled and very finely chopped
1 garlic clove, peeled and crushed
1 small stick of celery, strings removed and very finely chopped
*50 g	2 oz butter*
*450 g	1 lb spinach, cooked, drained and chopped*
salt and freshly ground black pepper
1 tsp Worcestershire sauce
24 freshly opened oysters on the half shell
3 tbsp breadcrumbs
1 tbsp fresh parsley

Preheat the oven to 230°C/450°F/gas mark 8. Put the spring onions, garlic, celery and butter in a frying pan and cook slowly for 10 minutes. Add the spinach, salt, pepper and Worcestershire sauce and stir well. Arrange the oysters on a baking tray and divide the spinach mixture among the oysters, spreading it round the rims of the shells and leaving the oysters glistening in the middle. Mix the breadcrumbs and parsley, then sprinkle over the oysters. Bake for 5–8 minutes or until the spinach is very hot, then serve.

SERVES 4 / /🐚🐚

French Mushroom Tartlets

This recipe began as a mistake. I asked a new cook to make baby mushroom quiches and this is what happened – a perfect mistake, and we have added to it and used it ever since. Make the tartlet cases on a rainy day and store in an air-tight tin. When baking blind, I do not line with greaseproof paper and beans or rice, but instead, half-way through cooking, take the tartlet cases out of the oven, pat them down flat with a cloth over my fingers and return them to the oven for the final cooking. You can use button or flat mushrooms; flat will make a darker filling, perhaps not as attractive to some, but I think they have more flavour. Serve two tartlets per person on a bed of green lettuce and garnish with a few slices of tomato.

For the pastry:
*225 g	8 oz plain flour*
a pinch of salt
*125 g	4 oz butter or margarine*
1 dsp chopped parsley (optional)

For the mushroom filling:
1 small onion, peeled and finely chopped
*50 g	2 oz butter*
*125 g	4 oz mushrooms, wiped and finely chopped*
*50 g	2 oz flour*
*150 ml	5 fl oz milk*
2 tbsp white wine (or more)
salt and freshly ground black pepper
1 tsp fresh thyme or oregano, finely chopped

Preheat the oven to 200°C/400°F/gas mark 6. To make the pastry, put the flour, salt, fat and parsley, if using, into a blender and blend until it resembles breadcrumbs. With the machine on, gradually add 2–3 tbsp cold water until the mixture rolls into a ball. If you have no blender, put the flour, salt and fat in a bowl, then, using your fingertips, rub the mixture until it resembles breadcrumbs. Using a round-bladed knife, stir in the water until the mixture forms large lumps, then put flour on your hand and gather the dough together and knead until the sides of the bowl are clean. Roll out on a floured surface to about 3 mm / $^1/_8''$ thick, cut out rounds with a 7.5 cm / 3″ round cutter and place the rounds into a tartlet baking tray. Press in with with your fingertips. Repeat until all the pastry is used up. Bake in the oven for 10 minutes. Take out and, with a cloth over your fingers, flatten the pastry that has risen. Return to oven and bake for a further 5 minutes or until the pastry is light brown. Cool, then store in a tin until needed.

To make the mushroom filling, put the onion and butter in a frying pan or large saucepan and cook for 3 minutes or until the onion is soft. Add the mushrooms and cook for a further 5 minutes. Stirring continuously, add the flour, then gradually add the milk, white wine, seasoning and herbs. When ready to serve, spoon a little hot filling into each tartlet case and serve immediately.

SERVES 4 / ♠♠

Filo Pizzas

You might think that pizza is too heavy for a starter, but filo makes a lovely, crisp, light base for the topping suggested here. Alternatively, use toppings that you particularly favour.

1 × 400 g / 14 oz packet of filo pastry
125 g / 4 oz butter, melted
2 × 200 g / 7 oz packets of Mozzarella, in whey, drained and sliced
16 slices of salami, rind removed
8 tomatoes, skinned (optional) and sliced
125 g / 4 oz pitted black olives, sliced
4–6 sprigs of thyme
salt and freshly ground black pepper
a little olive oil

Preheat the oven to 200°C/400°F/gas mark 6. Unwrap the filo pastry. Cover the pastry you are not using with a damp cloth. Cut a sheet in half to make 2 squares or oblongs, depending on the pastry shape, brush with butter and then place another square on top diagonally and brush again. Repeat 6 times. Start again to make 8 bases. Bake for 15 minutes or until crisp and light brown. Remove and leave to cool. Top with slice of Mozarella, salami, tomatoes and olives, covering right to the edges. Crumble over the thyme, then season well. Dribble over some olive oil, then place under a hot grill for about 5 minutes or until hot and bubbling. Serve immediately.

SERVES 8 / ♠♠

Scallop Mousses with Asparagus Sauce

The most attractive and authentic way to serve scallop mousse is using their shells as a mould. I have added asparagus to the Hollandaise sauce but if it is out of season, it can be omitted. You can buy the shells at most seaside tourist shops but moulds or ramekins can be used until you go on your next bucket-and-spade holiday.

For the scallop mousse:

1 small onion, peeled and finely chopped
a little oil
8 scallops
*25 g	1 oz butter*
*25 g	1 oz flour*
*150 ml	5 fl oz milk*
a dash of Tabasco
2 tbsp white wine
2 eggs, separated
1 tbsp lemon juice
1 good tsp powdered gelatine
salt and freshly ground black pepper

For the asparagus sauce:

2 egg yolks
juice of 1 lemon
freshly ground black pepper
*225 g	8 oz butter*
10 medium-sized spears of fresh asparagus, cooked, plus a few extras, for garnish (optional)
fresh parsley, for garnish

For the mousse, fry the onion in a little oil for a few minutes until soft. Add the scallops and cook for a further few minutes. Blend in a blender until smooth. Melt the butter in a saucepan, add the flour, then stir in the milk, Tabasco, white wine, egg yolks and scallop mixture. Remove from the heat. Pour the lemon juice into a small saucepan and sprinkle over the gelatine. Leave to soak for 1 minute, then dissolve over a very low heat until transparent, pour into the sauce mixture and stir well. Season, then beat the egg whites until stiff and, using a metal spoon, fold into the mixture. Spoon into oiled shells or moulds, smooth over, place on a tray, then chill until set.

For the sauce, put the egg yolks, lemon juice and pepper into a blender. Melt the butter in a saucepan and, when bubbling and very hot, turn the blender to high and immediately pour in the bubbling butter. Keep on maximum speed for 30 seconds after the butter has been added. The mixture should be thick and creamy. Add the asparagus spears and blend again until smooth. Cool. Pour the sauce on each plate and turn out the mousses on top. Garnish with asparagus or parsley.

SERVES 7 / 🌢🌢🌢 / FREEZE MOUSSE IN SHELLS

Jerusalem Artichoke Mousses with Bacon

Jerusalem artichokes have a very distinct flavour and make a smooth, delicate starter. The crispy bacon is a good textural contrast, but remember to be sparing with the salt when seasoning the mousse. Try to buy large artichoke roots as they are easier to peel than small ones.

a little oil
450 g / 1 lb Jerusalem artichokes, peeled and roughly sliced
50 g / 2 oz butter
50 g / 2 oz flour
300 ml / 10 fl oz milk
2 eggs, separated
salt and freshly ground black pepper
juice of ½ lemon
1 heaped tsp gelatine
2 tbsp double cream
4 rashers of streaky bacon, rind removed

Oil 8 ramekins. Cook the artichokes in boiling salted water for about 15 minutes or until soft. Drain and purée. Melt the butter in a saucepan, stir in the flour and then the milk to make a smooth white sauce. Remove from the heat, add the egg yolks and season. Put the lemon juice into a small saucepan and sprinkle over the gelatine. Leave to soak for 1 minute. Whisk the egg whites until stiff. Heat the gelatine over a very low heat, then when transparent add to the artichoke mixture, stirring well. Fold in the double cream and finally the egg whites. Pour into the ramekins and chill for at least 4 hours. Grill the bacon rashers until very crisp, then chop finely. Drain on kitchen roll to remove excess fat. To serve, turn out the mousses onto 8 small plate and sprinkle over the bacon.

SERVES 8 / 🌢🌢

Smoked Salmon with Scrambled Egg

This is quite a rich starter but the combination of the two flavours is perfect. It also makes a very good lunch or supper dish. Do not add salt to the scrambled egg as the smoked salmon is salty. Serve with thin brown bread and butter.

*350 g	12 oz smoked salmon, thinly sliced*
6 eggs
*50 g	2 oz butter*
*150 ml	5 fl oz milk*
freshly ground black pepper
a little parsley, chopped (optional)

Divide the smoked salmon between 6 small plates. Put the remaining ingredients in a heavy-based, non-stick saucepan and stir continuously over a medium heat until the eggs start to cook. Reduce the heat and continue stirring until the mixture becomes creamy and nearly cooked to the consistency that you like. I like it creamy and still pourable, but some people prefer it to be almost bouncy. Take the saucepan off the heat early and keep stirring as the mixture continues cooking for about 1 minute. Spoon on top of the smoked salmon and serve immediately.

SERVES 6 / 🍶🍶

MAIN COURSES

Barbecued Lamb Chops

Lamb cooked in a barbecue sauce makes a pleasant change. This quick, easy-to-make sauce can also be used with spare ribs, chickens or hamburgers. I would serve it with crunchy, short-grain brown rice and a crispy green salad.

1 tbsp dark-brown sugar
1 tsp dried mustard
1 tbsp vinegar
½ tsp paprika
1 tbsp Worcestershire sauce
1 tbsp lemon juice
1 tbsp runny honey
6 large, lean chump chops, trimmed

Preheat the oven to 200°C/400°F/gas mark 6. Put all the ingredients except the chops in a bowl and mix well. Place the chops in a shallow, ovenproof dish and pour over the sauce, making sure each chop is thoroughly coated. Cook for about 30 minutes or until the chops are shiny and crispy. Reduce the heat to low until ready to save.

SERVES 6 / ♥

Bobotie

This is a delicious African version of moussaka and great for a party or supper dish. It won't spoil if left in a low oven for an hour or two. Serve it with Herb and Garlic Bread (see page 151) and the Iceberg, Avocado and Kiwi-Fruit Salad (see page 142).

1 tbsp oil
2 onions, peeled and chopped
2 tsp curry powder
900 g / 2 lb lean minced beef
¼ tsp ground cloves
1 tsp turmeric
1 tbsp vinegar
½ tsp ground nutmeg
1 tsp ground ginger
1 tbsp mango chutney or apricot jam
1 dsp brown sugar (optional)
salt and freshly ground black pepper
a little stock to moisten

For the topping:
2 eggs, beaten
150 ml / 5 fl oz milk

Preheat the oven to 190°C/375°F/gas mark 5. Heat the oil in a saucepan, add the onions and curry powder and cook slowly for 3 minutes to soften the onions. Add the mince and stir well. Add the remaining ingredients and stir again. Pour into an ovenproof dish and smooth over the top. Mix the eggs and milk, then pour over the meat mixture. Bake in the oven for 30 minutes or until the top is golden brown, then reduce the heat to low until ready to serve.

SERVES 6 / 🌶 / FREEZE

Sweet and Sour Chicken

This sauce is also very good with prawns, pork or lamb. It is quick to make and can be frozen in portion packs.

a little oil
1 onion, peeled and finely chopped
1 carrot, peeled and finely chopped
1 small green pepper, cored, deseeded and finely chopped
1 tsp tomato purée
1 tbsp vinegar
1 tbsp Soya sauce
*1 × 227g	8 oz tin of pineapple chunks*
4 chicken breasts, skinned

Preheat the oven to 200°C/400°F/gas mark 6. Pour a little oil in a frying pan and add the onion. Cook on a low heat for 3 minutes. Add the carrot and pepper and cook for a further 5 minutes, then add the tomato purée, vinegar, Soya sauce and pineapple, with a little of the juice. Simmer for about 10 minutes on a very low heat to infuse the flavours. Set aside. Place the chicken breasts in a baking try and pour over the sauce. Cover and cook in the oven for 30 minutes or until the chicken is done.

SERVES 4 / ● / FREEZE

Trout with Mustard Sauce

I first had this dish when I was travelling through France on a gourmet holiday, and because it was easy to cook and delicious it has remained on our menus ever since. Remove the heads and tails, if wished. If you prefer crisp-skinned trout, then grill them instead under a medium heat for about 10 minutes on each side. Your appetite can determine the size of trout you choose.

8 rainbow trout, gutted
2 lemons, sliced
2 bay leaves
2 tbsp white wine or water
1 dsp coarse-grain mustard
300 ml	10 fl oz double cream
salt and freshly ground black pepper

Preheat the oven to 180°C/375°F/gas mark 4. Place 2 or 3 slices of lemon inside each trout, then place them in a baking tray with bay leaves and wine or water. Cover and bake for 45 minutes or until cooked, and the eyes are white. Put the mustard and cream in a saucepan and gently heat through. Remove the head and tail, if wished, and transfer the trout to a serving dish. Pour over the sauce and serve.

SERVES 8 / 🍷

Chocolate Chilli con Carne

Adding chocolate makes a great talking point and it really does add a lovely, dark glaze and extra flavour. This is ideal for a casual party such as Guy Fawkes evening, served with baked potatoes and salads, and can be made in advance and frozen.

1 tbsp oil
1 onion, peeled and chopped
1 level tsp chilli powder
450 g	1 lb lean minced beef
2 × 295 g	10.4 oz cans of red kidney beans, drained
25 g	1 oz dark chocolate, grated
1 dsp tomato purée
salt and freshly ground black pepper
a little stock or red wine, to moisten

Heat the oil in a saucepan, add the onion and chilli powder and fry gently for 3 minutes

Russian-Doll Chicken Breasts (page 73) with broccoli and wild and white rice.

George Butler III Steaks (page 78).

Hare in Chocolate Sauce (page 85) with Red Cabbage (page 92).

Scallops in Pastry Shells (page 88).

Paella (page 86).

Belgian Waffles with Advocaat (page 96).

Excruciating Chocolate Pudding (page 95).

Spiced and Sliced Pears (page 103).

to soften the onion. Add the rest of the ingredients and stir well. Simmer over a low heat for 30 minutes, stirring occasionally. Keep warm in a low oven until needed.

SERVES 4 / 🔥 / FREEZE

Pork Chops with Orange and Apple

My mother introduced this to me many years ago and it has remained a favourite. It is easy to make and has a warming, spicy flavour. Cut four slices from the thickest part of the orange, leaving the peel on, then squeeze the juice from the two ends for the cornflour mix. Serve with fluffy mashed potatoes and a green vegetable.

a little oil
4 pork chops, trimmed
1 orange, sliced with skin on
1 cooking apple, sliced with skin on
8 whole cloves
*295 g	10.4 oz tin of condensed consommé*
1 dsp brown sugar
¼ tsp ground cinnamon
1 dsp cornflour
2 tbsp orange juice

Put the oil in a large frying pan, then brown the chops on both sides. Place a slice of orange, then apple, on top of each chop, and secure with 2 cloves. Add the consommé, sugar and cinnamon. Cover and cook gently for 20 minutes or until the chops are done. Transfer the chops to a warmed serving dish. Mix the cornflour and orange juice in a cup and pour into the pan juices. Stirring continuously, cook over a low heat until it thickens. Pour over the chops and serve.

SERVES 4 / 🔥

HOW TO CUT THE FRUIT

Pork Chops with Prunes and Marrons

This is a love-or-hate dish; for me, a lover of prunes and chestnuts, it's a real winner. Many people turn their noses up at the idea, but wherever I serve this, the plates are scraped clean!

*1 × 400 g	14 oz tin of prunes, stoned*
*1 × 400 g	14 oz tin of puréed marrons, unsweetened*
2 tbsp red wine
salt and freshly ground black pepper
6 pork chops, trimmed

Preheat the oven to 200°C/400°F/gas mark 6. Put the prunes (with their juice) in a blender, making sure there are no stones, with the marrons, red wine and seasoning, and blend for 1 minute. Place the chops in an ovenproof dish and pour over the prune mixture. Cover and cook for 1 hour or on until the chops are tender. Turn the oven temperature to low and leave until ready to serve.

SERVES 6 / 🍶

Vegetarian Crumble

This is not only good for a vegetarian but excellent as an 'ordinary' lunch or supper. You can use any vegetables, so try your favourites, but Gorgonzola, with its creamy texture and good flavour, is the best cheese.

3 carrots, peeled and sliced
2 small parsnips, peeled and sliced
1 small cauliflower, stalk removed and cut into florets
3 courgettes, top, tailed and sliced
3 tbsp oil
2 onions, peeled and sliced
*125 g	4 oz mushrooms, wiped and sliced*
*50 g	2 oz butter*
*50 g	2 oz flour*
*10 fl oz	300 ml milk*
*175 g	6 oz Gorgonzola, crumbled*
4 slices of bread, made into fine crumbs
*50 g	2 oz cheddar cheese, grated*
1 heaped tsp mixed herbs, chopped
salt and freshly ground black pepper

Preheat the oven to 190°C/375°F/gas mark 5. Bring a large pan of salted water to the boil, then add the carrots, parsnips, cauliflower and courgettes. Bring back to the boil, simmer for 5 minutes, drain, then return the vegetables to the pan. Heat the oil in a large frying pan, add the onions and cook on a low heat for 5 minutes. Add the mushrooms and cook for a further 5 minutes.

Heat the butter in a saucepan, stir in the flour, then gradually stir in the milk to make a smooth white sauce. Add the Gorgonzola and cook on a low heat until the cheese is melted. Mix the breadcrumbs, cheddar cheese and herbs in a bowl and season with salt and pepper. Add the onion mix to the carrot mix and then stir in the cheese sauce. Put into a shallow, ovenproof dish and top with the breadcrumb mix. Bake for 30 minutes or until the crumbs are slightly brown. Serve hot.

SERVES 6 / ❦ / FREEZE

Salmon Steaks with Honey and Ginger

A tasty change from the usual plain poached salmon, this is best left to marinate for a few hours before cooking, so the flavours permeate the flesh. Serve with new or mashed potatoes and a crisp green vegetable, such as baby green beans or mange tout. Instead of using salmon steaks cut through the back bone I prefer steaks cut from a fillet, so they have no bones. If you have a tame fishmonger you could ask him to do this.

*4 × 125–150 g	4–5 oz salmon steaks*
1 dsp runny honey
1 tsp freshly grated root ginger
rind of 1 orange
salt and freshly ground black pepper

Preheat the oven to 180°C/350°F/gas mark 4. Put the salmon steaks in an ovenproof dish. Put the honey, ginger and orange rind in a saucepan and heat gently. Stir well, cool slightly, then pour over the steaks. Cover and cook for about 20 minutes or until the steaks are just cooked; the flesh should flake easily and the juices should be steaming. Serve immediately.

SERVES 4 / ❦

Salmon Steaks with Bacon and Rosemary

Here, salmon steaks are brought to the table wrapped up in parcels for each guest to unwrap. I have not added salt because of the bacon but, depending on how salty it is, you may need to add a little later.

a little butter
4 × 125–150 g | 4–5 oz salmon steaks
4 rashers of back bacon, rind removed and finely chopped
freshly ground black pepper
4 sprigs of fresh rosemary

Preheat the oven to 180°C / 350°F / gas mark 4. Butter the middle of 4 × 30 cm / 12″ squares of greaseproof paper, then lay a steak in the centre of each piece. Cover each steak with bacon, grind over some pepper, then place a sprig of rosemary on top. Wrap each parcel up well, tucking the flaps underneath, and place on a baking tray. Cook for 15–20 minutes or until each parcel is steaming hot.

SERVES 4 / 🖑

Bass with Tomato and Basil Sauce

When I was a child and October came round, we used to hire a boat from St Anthony, near Helford in Cornwall, go out to sea and catch huge sea bass. That was the easy bit. We would then come back, dig a hole on the beach, light a fire in the hole, place the bass wrapped in foil in the hole, then cover it up. After two hours the bass was cooked but the problem was that, after a few drinks, the hole seemed to have moved and quite often dinner was lost. Instead of bass, you can use cod, a very underrated fish.

8 × 125–150g | 4–5 oz bass or cod fillets
For the sauce:
1 medium-sized onion, peeled and chopped
1 garlic clove, peeled and crushed (optional)
1 tbsp olive oil
6 tomatoes
a handful of fresh basil
½ tsp caster sugar
salt and freshly ground black pepper

Preheat the oven to 180°C/350°F/gas mark 4. Put the onion, garlic and oil in a small frying pan and fry gently for 5 minutes. Make a small nick in the skin of each tomato. Bring a small saucepan of water to the boil, then add the tomatoes. Leave for a few seconds or until the skin splits where cut. Drain, run under cold water, then remove the skins. Place all the ingredients in a blender except the fish and blend until puréed. Pour the sauce into an ovenproof dish and lay the fish on top. Cover and bake for 25 minutes or until the fish is cooked.

SERVES 8 / 🍾🍾

Stuffed Leg of Lamb

This is one of my favourite roasts. Ask the butcher to remove the bones; this makes the leg possible to stuff and wonderful to carve. The flavours from the stuffing permeate the flesh during the cooking and the marmalade gives the skin a toffee texture.

2 tbsp virgin olive oil
1 garlic clove, peeled and crushed
1 × 1.75 kg	4 lb leg of lamb, boned
1 onion, peeled and finely chopped
6 tbsp brown breadcrumbs
1 dsp redcurrant jelly
grated rind and juice of 1 orange
salt and freshly ground black pepper
1 tsp chopped rosemary
50 g	2 oz dried apricots, finely chopped (optional)
1 tbsp marmalade

Preheat the oven to 200°C/400°F/gas mark 6. Mix 1 tbsp olive oil and garlic, then spread over the inside of the lamb. Fry the onion in the remaining oil, then mix all the ingredients except the marmalade and stuff into the hollow lamb, securing it with skewers or kebab sticks. Place in a roasting tin, spread the marmalade over the skin and roast for 1 hour. Reduce the oven temperature to 180°C/375°F/gas mark 4 and cook for a further 30–60 minutes, according to how well done you like your meat. Place the joint on a serving dish, remove the skewers or sticks and keep warm until ready to carve. Strain the fat off the juices and serve them as gravy.

SERVES 6–8 / 🍾🍾

Chicken Divan

This is an old, war-time recipe; I use broccoli rather than the traditional spinach, but you can easily change it back if you wish. The meat is portioned and therefore easy to serve at a dinner party. You do not need to warm the milk for the sauce but it does make it faster and easier.

50 g / 2 oz butter
50 g / 2 oz flour
450 ml / 15 fl oz milk, warmed
4 tbsp sherry
2 tsp Worcestershire sauce
freshly ground black pepper
150 ml / 5 fl oz double cream, lightly whipped
675 g / 1½ lb broccoli, blanched
6 chicken breasts, skinned and boned

Preheat the oven to 180°C/350°F/gas mark 4. Melt the butter in a saucepan, add the flour and stir in the milk to make a smooth sauce. Add the sherry, Worcestershire sauce, pepper and then fold in the cream. Lay the broccoli in a buttered, ovenproof dish and then place the chicken breasts on top. Pour over the sauce and bake for 40 minutes or until slightly brown on top and thoroughly cooked.

SERVES 6 / 🌭🌭

Chicken Majorca

I am a great fan of fruit and meat combinations and this is even more interesting, with the extra flavours of the olives and the colourful red peppers. You can buy two whole chickens and quarter them but buying quarters is easier and you can choose as many legs or breasts as you wish.

1 tbsp olive oil
1 onion, peeled and chopped
8 chicken quarters
2 tbsp flour
200 ml / 7 fl oz milk
200 ml / 7 fl oz white wine
1 tsp oregano
salt and freshly ground black pepper
125 g / 4 oz pitted green olives, halved
1 red pepper, cored, deseeded and chopped
2 oranges, peeled like an apple and segmented

Preheat the oven to 180°C/350°F/gas mark 4. Put the oil in a large casserole, then add the onion. Fry gently for 5 minutes, then add the chicken pieces, 4 at a time, and brown on each side. Set the chicken aside and stir the flour into the juices. Stir in the milk and wine to make the sauce, then add the oregano, seasoning, olives, pepper and oranges. Mix well and replace the chicken pieces, making sure they are coated with the sauce. Cover and cook for 1 hour or until the chicken is done, then keep in a very low oven until ready to serve.

SERVES 8 / ♦♦ / FREEZE

Chicken Curry

Curries are 'fun' party food, especially with all their accompaniments. Serve with rice cooked in a little saffron or turmeric to give a good yellow colour, and pour yourself a glass of cool lager.

1 dsp fresh root ginger, grated
2 garlic cloves, peeled and crushed
2 tbsp ground almonds
3 tbsp oil
*1 × 1.75 kilo	4 lb chicken, jointed*
5 whole cardamom pods
*1 × 2.5 cm	1" cinnamon stick or ½ tsp cinnamon powder*
2 bay leaves
5 whole cloves or ½ tsp ground cloves
1 tsp Garam masala
1 onion, peeled and chopped
1 tsp ground cumin
a pinch of cayenne pepper
*250 g	9 oz natural yogurt*
1 tbsp sultanas

To accompany:

¼ cucumber, peeled and thinly sliced
2 tbsp soured cream
2 bananas, peeled and sliced
2 tbsp salted peanuts
12 popadoms, cooked as instructed on packet
mango chutney

Preheat the oven to 160°C/325°F/gas mark 3. Put the ginger, garlic, ground almonds and 2 tbsp water in a casserole and mix well with a spoon. Heat the oil in a large, ovenproof casserole, add the chicken pieces and brown on all sides. Add the remaining ingredients and stir well. Cover and bake for 1 hour or until the chicken is cooked. For the accompaniments, mix the cucumber and soured cream together and put in a small bowl. Serve the other ingredients, each in a separate bowl.

SERVES 4–5 / ❦❦ FREEZE

Russian-Doll Chicken Breasts

This gets its name from the many layers built up outside and inside the central core of chicken. I am not usually so keen on many different flavours in one dish, but this works very well. If you wish, you can omit the pastry, but in that case cover the baking tray with foil to prevent the chicken drying out.

4 chicken breasts, skinned and boned
*125 g	4 oz Gorgonzola cheese*
4 asparagus spears, blanched
freshly ground black pepper
4 slices of Parma ham
8 sheets of filo pastry
*50 g	2 oz butter, melted*

Preheat the oven to 190°C/375°F/gas mark 5. Lay open the chicken breasts to reveal the small flap, or cut a small flap, and stuff each one with a quarter of the cheese. Place an asparagus spear on the cheese, season with pepper and close each breast. Wrap each breast with a slice of Parma ham. Unfold the filo pastry and brush 2 sheets with the melted butter. Place 1 sheet on top of the other, wrap up a chicken breast like a parcel, then brush again on the outside with melted butter. Place on a baking tray and repeat with the other breasts. Bake for 30 minutes or until the pastry is golden brown. Serve immediately.

SERVES 4 / ♦♦

Gammon with Sugar and Spice

A very traditional English dish, this is best cooked firstly by simmering to keep it moist and give it a good apple and herb flavour and then by roasting for a wonderful, sticky coating. I like it with Red Cabbage (see page 92), fluffy mashed potato and Cumberland Sauce (see page 156).

1 × 1.4 kilo / 3 lb piece of middle-cut gammon
1 small onion, peeled and quartered
3 bay leaves
600 ml / 1 pint apple juice or cider
20 whole cloves
1 tbsp marmalade
2 tbsp dark-brown sugar

Put the gammon in a saucepan, cover with water, bring to the boil, then drain. Return the meat to the saucepan, then add the onion, bay leaves, apple juice or cider and half the cloves, plus water to cover the meat, if not covered. Cover, bring to the boil, then simmer for 45 minutes, Leave to cool in the liquid until ready to roast.

Preheat the oven to 200°C/400°F/gas mark 6. Remove the gammon from the pan, drain, then, using a sharp knife, strip away the rind, leaving the layer of white fat. Score the fat in a criss-cross fashion, then spread with the marmalade, pat on the sugar and, finally, spear the cloves evenly over the roast. Place in a roasting tin in the oven and cook for 35 minutes or until the skin has a caramel texture. Remove, cool slightly, carve and serve.

SERVES 6–8 / 👆👆

Beef Carbonnade

Beef cooked in beer has a nutty flavour – and is especially good for a winter buffet party, served with rice and salads. Chuck steak is fine but make sure you remove all the gristle and fat; a friendly butcher might prepare it for you, which saves time when cooking for a large number of people. The easiest way to coat the meat with flour is to put the flour in a plastic bag, add the meat and toss well, leaving air in the bag and holding the top tightly shut – for obvious reasons!

a little oil
2 onions, peeled and chopped
2 garlic cloves, peeled and crushed
*900 g	2 lb chuck steak, cut into 2.5 cm	1" cubes*
2–3 tbsp flour
1 tbsp soft brown sugar
*300 ml	10 fl oz stout or brown ale*
1 bouquet garni
2 bay leaves (fresh, if possible)
salt and freshly ground black pepper
a little stock or extra beer if necessary
2 slices of brown bread
1 tbsp coarse-grain mustard
chopped parsley

Preheat the oven to 160°C/325°F/gas mark 3. Heat the oil in a heavy-based casserole, add the onions and garlic and fry for 5 minutes or until the onion is soft. Coat the meat in flour, add to the casserole and brown slightly. Add the sugar, stout or ale, herbs and seasoning. Stir, cover and cook for 1–1½ hours or until the meat is tender. Remove the bay leaves and bouquet garni, squeezing the juice into the casserole. Add extra liquid if necessary but sauce should be quite thick. Turn the oven to low until ready to serve. Meanwhile, toast the bread, quarter into triangles and spread with mustard. Serve garnished with the chopped parsley and toast triangles.

SERVES 4–6 / ♦♦ / FREEZE

George Butler III Steaks

I was given this steak twenty-two years ago when I was staying in New Orleans and still remember it as if it were yesterday, it was so good. You could marinate it the night before and then just grill it at the last moment. Adjust the grilling time according to how thick the steaks are and how well cooked you like your meat. If you are in a hurry, forget the marinade and just do the topping.

3 tbsp red wine
1 garlic clove, peeled and crushed
2 bay leaves
juice of ½ lemon
freshly ground black pepper
4 fillet steaks
1 dsp dark brown sugar
1 dsp French or coarse-grain mustard

Put the wine, garlic, bay leaves, lemon juice and pepper in a bowl and mix well. Place the steaks in a shallow, glazed or glass dish, then pour over the marinade. Cover and chill for a few hours, turning the meat once. Preheat the grill to very hot. Grill the steaks for approximately 2–3 minutes or until the sugar is slightly caramelised. Serve immediately.

SERVES 4 / 👫

ident'

sen son,

his life

Lamb with Port and Orange

Casseroles can be considered too dull for a dinner party, but this one is very popular. For a stronger orange flavour use the rind but instead of the fresh orange juice, use half a carton of condensed, frozen orange juice. If you wish to use a cheaper cut of meat, buy 1.4 kilo | 3 lb of lamb neck fillets.

1 small leg of lamb
1 onion, peeled and finely chopped
1 tbsp oil
2 tbsp flour
salt and freshly ground black pepper
grated rind and juice of 1 orange
1 dsp redcurrant jelly
1 tsp rosemary, finely chopped
1 wine-glass of port
a little red wine or stock, if necessary

Preheat the oven to 150°C/300°F/gas mark 2. Cut the meat off the bone, then dice. Put the onion and oil in a heavy-based casserole and fry over a low heat for a few minutes or until soft. Add the meat and brown slightly. Stir in the flour. Add the remaining ingredients and enough red wine or stock to give a tacky mixture. Cover and cook for 2 hours, stirring occasionally and adding more liquid if necessary, then serve.

SERVES 4–6 / 🍶🍶 / FREEZE

Moussaka

This famous Greek recipe is a convenient lunch party or supper dish, since it can be cooked in advance and frozen. You can use either lamb or beef but it is essential to use thyme, rosemary and olive oil, which are typical Greek ingredients. If the aubergines are small, there is no need to salt them. Serve with mixed leaf salad and Herb and Garlic Bread (see page 151).

*675 g	1½ lb aubergines, thinly sliced*
salt and freshly ground black pepper
*150 ml	5 fl oz olive oil*
*50 g	2 oz butter*
1 large onion, peeled and chopped
2 garlic cloves, peeled and crushed
*900 g	2 lb lean, minced lamb*
1 tbsp tomato purée
1 tsp fresh thyme, chopped
1 tsp fresh rosemary, finely chopped
3 tbsp red wine
For the topping:
4 eggs
*300 ml	10 fl oz single cream*
*300 ml	10 fl oz natural yogurt*

Sprinkle the aubergine slices with salt to remove the bitter juices. After 10 minutes, rinse, then pat dry with kitchen roll. Heat some of the oil in a large frying pan and fry the aubergine on both sides until brown, adding more oil as necessary. (You may need extra oil.) Remove and set aside. Heat 25 g / 1 oz butter in a large saucepan, then cook the onion and garlic for 3 minutes over a low heat. Add the mince, stir well to brown, then add the tomato purée, herbs, salt and pepper and then red wine. Stir well and cook gently for 5 minutes. Preheat the oven to 200°C/400°F/gas mark 6. Butter a deep, ovenproof dish and put in half the mince mixture, then cover with half the aubergine slices. Repeat again, using up all the ingredients. Mix the eggs, cream and yogurt and pour over the top. Bake for 45 minutes or until the top is golden brown. Turn down the oven to low until ready to serve.

SERVES 6 / ♦♦ / FREEZE

Oxtail Casserole

This is a much-forgotten English dish, really delicious on a cold winter's day. It is best cooked the day before and cooled so that the fat can be removed. The longer it cooks, the better it tastes.

*1 large oxtail, cut into approx 5 cm	2" pieces*
a little flour
salt and freshly ground black pepper
2 tbsp oil
1 large onion, peeled and finely chopped
*300 ml	10 fl oz red wine*
1 bouquet garni
2 bay leaves
1 tbsp redcurrant jelly
grated rind of 1 lemon
*225 g	8 oz carrots, peeled and chopped*
1 small turnip, peeled and chopped
1 dsp tomato purée
*175 g	6 oz mushrooms, wiped and sliced*
chopped parsley

Preheat the oven to 140°C/275°F/gas mark 1. Coat the oxtail in the flour with salt and pepper. Heat the oil in a large, ovenproof casserole, add the onion, then fry gently for 3 minutes. Add the oxtail, then brown on all sides. Pour in the wine and 6 tbsp water, then add the bouquet garni, bay leaves, redcurrant jelly and lemon rind. Stir well, then heat for about 5 minutes. Cover, then cook in the oven for 2 hours. Remove from the oven, stir well and add more water if necessary. Add the carrots, turnip, tomato purée and mushrooms and stir again. Cover and then cook for a further 1½ hours. Remove from the oven, remove the bouquet garni and leave overnight if possible. When cold, remove the layer of fat from the top, preheat the oven to the same temperature and reheat for 1 hour. Garnish, then serve.

SERVES 4–6 / ♦♦ / FREEZE

Pheasant in Apple and Somerset Cider Brandy

I used to live in pheasant country in Somerset, and was always being asked for different ways of cooking these birds. This recipe linked in nicely with the locally made cider brandy.

1 pheasant, oven ready
salt and freshly ground black pepper
50 g / 2 oz butter
1 onion, peeled and finely chopped
½ tsp chopped thyme
1 cooking apple, peeled, cored and chopped
a good dash of Somerset Royal or Calvados brandy
150 ml / 5 fl oz double cream

Preheat the oven to 180°C/350°F/gas mark 4. Put the pheasant in a roasting tin, add 15 mm / ½″ water and season with salt and pepper. Cover tightly and roast for 45 minutes or until the bird is cooked. Remove from the oven and leave to cool. Melt the butter in a saucepan and cook the onion and thyme for 5 minutes or until the onion is soft but not brown. Add the apple and cook for a further 3 minutes. Stir in the juices from the cavity of the pheasant, the brandy and the cream. Stir well and remove from the heat. Joint the pheasant and place in the sauce. Reheat over a low heat and serve.

SERVES 3–4 / 🌢🌢 / FREEZE

Layered Polenta

When I was in Venice a long time ago I met an Italian couple on a vaporetto and, after chatting for a while, I ended up having dinner with them at their home. They cooked a variation of this dish which, when I came back to England, I tried to re-create. It makes a good main course, served with a leaf salad and Herb and Garlic Bread (see page 151). Polenta, or ground cornmeal, can be bought in health food shops and some supermarkets and, if you feel adventurous, use various wild mushrooms such as boletus, to add extra flavour.

4 tbsp olive oil
1 onion, peeled and finely chopped
225 g / 8 oz button mushrooms, wiped and sliced
300 ml / 10 fl oz half water and half milk
225 g / 8 oz polenta

| salt and freshly ground black pepper |
| 8 thinly cut slices of garlic salami (optional) |
| 175 g / 6 oz Gorgonzola, thinly sliced |
| 3 tomatoes, sliced |
| 75 g / 3 oz cheddar cheese |

Preheat the oven to 190°C/375°F/gas mark 5. Put 2 tablespoons of the oil in a frying pan with the onion and cook over a low heat for 5 minutes or until soft but not brown, then add the mushrooms. Fry for a further 5 minutes or until the mushrooms are cooked. Put 750 ml / 1¼ pt water and the milk into a saucepan and bring to the boil. Whisk in the polenta and cook over a low heat for 1 minute, stirring continuously. Add the remaining olive oil and seasoning. Put half the polenta into a deep 22.5 cm / 9″ diameter, ovenproof dish and evenly spoon the mushroom mixture on top. Cover with a layer of salami, if using, then the Gorgonzola. Smooth over the remaining polenta, cover with a layer of tomatoes and finally sprinkle over the cheddar cheese. Bake for 40 minutes or until light brown on top. Turn the oven to low until ready to serve.

SERVES 6 / ♠♠

Stuffed Quail

Now that quail are farmed, they are widely available, but not many cookbooks seem to include them. At some shops you can buy boned birds, which are certainly easier to eat but, boned or not, they look smart at a dinner table served hot on nests of Wild and Brown Rice (see page 94).

| 1 small onion, peeled and finely chopped |
| 1 tbsp olive oil |
| 4 tbsp breadcrumbs |
| 1 tsp mixed herbs |
| salt and freshly ground black pepper |
| 125 g / 4 oz shelled pistachio nuts, chopped |
| 8 oven-ready quail |
| 150 ml / 5 fl oz red wine |

Preheat the oven to 200°C/400°F/gas mark 6. Fry the onion in the olive oil for 5 minutes, then add the breadcrumbs, herbs, seasoning and nuts. (If the pistachios are salty, omit the salt.) Stir well, then stuff the quails with the mixture. Place the birds in a roasting tin, pour over the red wine, then cover and cook for 20 minutes. Remove the cover and cook for a further 10 minutes. Serve immediately to prevent the breasts drying out, using the juice as gravy.

SERVES 4 / ♠♠

Ugli Duckling

One of the main 'attractions' of this recipe is its name but it is delicious as well, and less fatty than most duck recipes. If you cannot buy ugli fruit, use sweet pink grapefruit. Peel them like an apple, cutting round with a sharp knife and removing the pith as well as the skin, then cut in between each segment and discard the core section. Serve with herb rice and petits pois.

1 × 2.8 kilo / 6 lb duck
50 g / 2 oz butter
50 g / 2 oz flour
2 ugli fruit or pink grapefruit, peeled and segmented
1 dsp fresh thyme, chopped
salt and freshly ground black pepper
a good splash of white wine
3 tbsp double cream
sugar (optional)

Preheat the oven to 200°C/400°F/gas mark 6. Prick the duck skin all over with a fork, to allow the fat to escape and baste the bird. Place in a roasting tin and roast for about 2 hours or until the duck is thoroughly cooked and no blood appears when speared with a skewer down the inside of the leg. Leave to cool, then cut the flesh into bite-sized pieces. Put the bones in a large saucepan and cover with hot water. Bring to the boil, simmer for

HOW TO PEEL AND SEGMENT THE FRUIT

about 30 minutes, then strain, discarding the bones. Melt the butter in a saucepan, stir in the flour, and about 600 ml / 1 pint stock to make a sauce. Add the ugli fruit or grapefruit segments, thyme, seasoning, white wine and cream. Stir in the duck meat, gently heat and serve. Alternatively, leave in a low oven until needed.

SERVES 4 / 🍷🍷 / FREEZE

Hare in Chocolate Sauce

Yes, a strange mixture but it works very well. I served this dish to a very conservative friend and then when his plate was empty I told him what he had eaten. He would not have touched it if he had known, but he had enjoyed it. Hare has a strong taste, while the chocolate adds a subtle flavour and gives the sauce a lovely shine. It is best to marinate the hare pieces overnight to allow all the flavours to permeate the flesh, so you will need to start a day in advance. Serve with mashed potato and a green vegetable, such as broccoli, to balance the richness of the hare.

a little oil
1 large onion, peeled and chopped
2 garlic cloves, peeled and crushed
1 × 2.3 kilo / 5 lb hare, jointed
1 stick of celery, washed, strings removed, and chopped finely
1 large carrot, peeled and finely chopped
3 bay leaves
300 ml / 10 fl oz red wine
salt and freshly ground black pepper
a little flour
50 g / 2 oz dark chocolate, grated

Heat the oil in a frying pan and cook the onion and garlic for 5 minutes or until soft but not brown. Place the hare joints in a bowl with onion mix, celery, carrot, bay leaves, wine and seasoning. Cover and refrigerate overnight.

Preheat the oven to 180°C/350°F/gas mark 4. Remove the hare pieces from the marinade, then coat with flour. Place in a large, heavy-based casserole and pour over the marinade. Cover and cook for about 2½ hours or until the hare is tender. Stir in the grated chocolate, remove the bay leaves, if wished, and serve.

SERVES 6–8 / 🍷🍷 / FREEZE

Special Fish Pie

This started off as quite an ordinary fish pie but through the years, clients and cooks have added more. Now is the time to stop adding. This is excellent for a party but if people are standing and eating, then change the top to mashed potato, as it is easier to eat. I have chosen smoked cod rather than smoked haddock as there are fewer bones. If cooking for vegetarians, omit the bacon. The pie will keep for up to an hour in a low oven.

450 g / 1 lb smoked cod
600 ml / 1 pint milk
1 onion, peeled and finely chopped
5 rashers of streaky bacon, rind removed and chopped
50 g / 2 oz butter
50 g / 2 oz flour
2 hard-boiled eggs, shelled and chopped
juice of 1 lemon
1 red pepper, cored, deseeded and finely chopped
1 tsp dried mustard
a few drops of Tabasco
2 tbsp chopped parsley
125 g / 4 oz frozen cockles, thawed and drained
125 g / 4 oz frozen mussels, thawed and drained
125 g / 4 oz frozen shelled prawns, thawed
freshly ground black pepper
1 × 375 g / 13 oz packet of puff pastry

For the glaze:

1 egg
1 tbsp milk

Preheat the oven to 200°C/400°F/gas mark 6. Put the cod in a saucepan with the milk, bring to the boil, cover and simmer for 5 minutes. Remove from the heat and strain, reserving the milk. Fry the onion and bacon for 5 minutes and set aside. Melt the butter in a saucepan, add the flour and, stirring continuously, slowly add the strained milk to make a smooth sauce. Remove the bones from the fish and flake. Add the remaining ingredients except the pastry to the sauce and stir well. Pour into a 30 cm / 12" diameter deep pie dish. Roll out the pastry to cover the dish, wet the edges of the dish, then lay the pastry over the top. Trim the pastry edges, then press down carefully with a fork. If you wish, cut out shapes from the left-over pastry, then place them on the top of the pie. Mix the egg and milk for the glaze and brush the pastry well. Bake for 30 minutes or until golden on top, reduce the heat to low until ready to serve.

SERVES 8 / ❦❦ / FREEZE

A FEW FAVOURITE VEGETABLES

Hot Beetroot in White Sauce

Bought cooked beetroots are, to my mind, unacceptable but, prepared this way, the beetroot is sweet and full of flavour and the sauce turns a lovely, deep-red colour – which in my case matches the dining-room walls to perfection!

450 g / 1 lb uncooked beetroot, with 2.5 cm / 1" of stalks attached
salt and freshly ground black pepper
50 g / 2 oz butter
50 g / 2 oz flour
300 ml / 10 fl oz milk

Put the beetroot in a saucepan, cover with water and add salt. Cover and bring to the boil, reduce the heat, then simmer for 1 hour. Drain and, when the beetroots are cool, remove the skins and cut into 2.5 cm / 1" cubes. Melt the butter in a small saucepan, add the flour to make a roux and then stir in the milk to make a smooth white sauce. Season with salt and pepper. Add the warm beetroot cubes and mix well. Serve hot.

SERVES 4 / 🍶

Celeriac and Carrot Purée

I add the carrot for colour more than for flavour, as the celeriac has such a creamy, full taste of its own. Use a blender for a really smooth result.

900 g / 2 lb celeriac, peeled and cut into 2.5 cm / 1" cubes
1 carrot, peeled and sliced
salt and freshly ground black pepper
75 ml / 3 fl oz double cream
50 g / 2 oz butter

Put the celeriac and carrot in a saucepan, add salt, cover with water and bring to the boil. Reduce the heat and simmer for 20 minutes or until the celeriac is soft. Drain and put into a blender. Add pepper, cream and butter and blend until smooth and fluffy. Put in an ovenproof dish, cover and keep warm until ready to serve.

SERVES 6–8 / 🍶

Red Cabbage

Because this recipe takes a long time to cook, I always double the quantity and freeze half. It is good reheated and, the more it is cooked, the better the taste. Dripping is not essential but it certainly adds flavour. Use the fat from a recent roast, if possible, or lard. Serve with game or gammon.

25 g | 1 oz dripping or lard
1 onion, peeled and finely chopped
900 g | 2 lb red cabbage, chopped into 2.5 cm | 1" pieces
1 cooking apple, peeled, cored and chopped
50 g | 2 oz sultanas
½ tsp cinnamon powder
1 garlic clove, peeled and crushed
2 tbsp brown sugar
salt and freshly ground black pepper

Melt the dripping or lard in a heavy-based saucepan. Add the onion and cook gently for 3 minutes or until soft. Add the rest of the ingredients, stir well, cover and cook over a very low heat for about 3 hours, stirring occasionally. Do not let it burn or 'catch' on the bottom.

SERVES 8–10 / ●● / FREEZE

Mashed Potatoes with Olive Oil

When I feel in the mood for comfort food, this is ideal with some crispy bacon on top. There are many kinds of potato, so choose a good, fluffy, mashing variety; check on the packet or ask your greengrocer, if necessary.

675 g | 1½ lb potatoes, peeled and chopped
1 small onion, peeled and chopped
salt and freshly ground black pepper
75 ml | 3 fl oz milk
75 ml | 3 fl oz virgin olive oil
freshly grated nutmeg

Put the potatoes and onion in a saucepan, cover with water, add salt, then bring to the boil. Reduce the heat and simmer for about 20 minutes or until the potatoes are soft. Drain and return to the saucepan. Mash the potatoes and onions, adding the milk gradually, then enough oil to get the consistency you like. Check the seasoning. Beat well to make fluffy and white. Put in an ovenproof dish, grate over nutmeg and keep warm until ready to serve.

SERVES 4–6 / ●

Jack Pots!

These are so much better than plain baked spuds, that they are well worth the effort. They can be prepared in advance and then heated under a medium grill or put into a medium oven for 20 minutes to warm through.

6–8 medium-sized baking potatoes, washed
oil
salt and freshly ground black pepper
*125 g	4 oz butter*
a little milk
*125 g	4 oz cheddar cheese, grated*

Preheat the oven to 200°C/400°F/gas mark 6. Using your hands, rub a little oil and salt on the potato skins and then prick them with a fork. Place on a baking tray or thread onto long skewers. Bake for 1 hour or until the skins are crisp and the potatoes are cooked. Cut in half lengthways. Holding the hot potato half in a cloth in one hand, scoop out the flesh with a dessertspoon into a flat-bottomed bowl or saucepan, then add the butter and, gradually, the milk, salt and pepper, mashing until light and fluffy. Spoon the mash into the empty jackets and put them onto a grill pan or in an ovenproof dish. Sprinkle over the cheese and grill or return to the oven for a few minutes.

SERVES 6–8 / ♦♦

Baked Sweet Potatoes

With my sweet tooth and my memories of steel bands blasting past at the Trinidad Carnival, these have to be one of my favourite vegetables. A few years ago, you could only buy them in street markets, but now most supermarkets stock them. After the potatoes are cooked, you can also cut them in half, sprinkle over some dark-brown sugar and put them under a very hot grill for 3 minutes, or until caramelised and bubbling.

8 small, or 4 large, sweet potatoes, washed and halved if large
a little oil
*50 g	2 oz butter*
salt and freshly ground black pepper
freshly ground nutmeg

Preheat the oven to 200°C/400°F/gas mark 6. Rub the potatoes in a little oil, then place on a baking tray. Bake for 1 hour or until soft. Remove from the oven, cut in half and butter each half. Season with salt and pepper and then grind over some fresh nutmeg. Mix lightly with a fork, then serve.

SERVES 8 / ♦

Wild and Brown Rice

This is not strictly a vegetable, I know, but it makes a delicious accompaniment to all sorts of main courses, so I am including it here. If you are feeling lavish, you can use wild rice on its own but as it is expensive I mix it with brown rice for a bit of padding and contrasting texture. The wild rice has a wonderful, nutty crunchiness and a deep-brown colour and looks great coated in a little shining armour of oil.

*225 g	8 oz wild rice*
*225 g	8 oz brown rice*
salt and freshly ground black pepper
1 small onion, peeled and finely chopped
2 tbsp oil
1 tbsp chopped parsley

Put the wild rice into a saucepan, cover generously with water then add salt. Bring to the boil, add the brown rice, reduce the heat and simmer for about 25 minutes or according to packet instructions, until the rice is cooked. Drain. Put the onion and oil in the saucepan and cook over a low heat for 5 minutes or until the onion is soft but not brown. Add the rice and season again. Stir in the parsley and serve.

SERVES 6–8 / ❦

PUDDINGS

Excruciating Chocolate Pudding

There is nothing quite like this pudding for flavour and for richness. Served hot from the oven with double cream, it must be the nearest thing to heaven – or hell, if you finish it! It can be made in advance and then warmed again in a low oven. A wonderful childhood memory – thank you, Mum.

*50 g	2 oz butter*
*50 g	2 oz plain chocolate*
*125 g	4 oz self-raising flour*
1 heaped tsp baking powder
*175 g	6 oz caster sugar*
*150 ml	5 fl oz milk*
*50 g	2 oz sugar*
*50 g	2 oz soft dark-brown sugar*
2 heaped tbsp cocoa powder

Preheat the oven to 180°C/350°F/gas mark 4. Put the butter and chocolate in a small basin in a saucepan of water and melt over a very low heat. Put the flour, baking powder and caster sugar in a bowl, stir in the butter, chocolate and milk, then beat until smooth. Put into an ovenproof, shallow dish. Mix the sugar, dark-brown sugar and cocoa powder in a cup and sprinkle over the top of the pudding mixture. Pour over 150 ml / 5 fl oz of water, then carefully place in the oven and cook for about 45 minutes or until the top is firm and crispy but the bottom is still gooey and fudge-like.

SERVES 6–8 / ♦ / FREEZE

Flambéed Bananas

Anyone can pretend to be a flamboyant chef with this recipe but mind your eyelashes! This is a great favourite of mine because there is no preparation beforehand and you can use up any odd drinks brought back from various holidays.

25 g / 1 oz butter
1 tbsp dark-brown sugar
6 bananas, peeled and cut in half lengthways
4 tbsp liqueur such as brandy, rum or Grand Marnier
300 ml / 10 fl oz double cream, whipped

Melt the butter and sugar in a large, heavy-based frying pan. When melted, reduce the heat, then add the bananas. Cook for 1 minute, turn up the heat to medium, then pour in the alcohol. Turn up the heat to maximum, stand back and set alight. When the flames die down, transfer 2 banana halves to each plate, pour over the juices, then serve with whipped double cream.

SERVES 6 / ♠

Belgian Waffles with Advocaat

When my number-one cook turned twenty-one, we went on a surprise trip to Bruges, a city of gastronomic delights. After a huge lunch and before a substantial dinner, we were tempted into a café and discovered this superb 'teatime snack'! It is very easy and a hit at every dinner party. When strawberries are in season, they make a good alternative to the bananas.

4 waffles
300 ml / 10 fl oz double cream, whipped
4 small bananas, peeled
4 tbsp Advocaat
icing sugar
mint leaves

Grill or toast the waffles until golden brown and crisp on both sides. Place on a dessert plate, spoon a quarter of the whipped cream on each, slice a banana on top, then pour over one tablespoon of Advocaat. Sift over some icing sugar, garnish with mint leaves and serve immediately.

SERVES 4 / ♠

Kinky Pie (page 106).

Brown Bread Ice-Cream with Strawberries (page 108).

Tiramisu (page 104).

Meringue Roulade (page 113).

Chestnut Meringue Cake (page 114).

Jack Hawkins' Cheesecake (page 116) with Caramelised Clementines (page 99).

Beignets with Lemon Sauce (page 121).

Floating Islands (page 126).

Ice-Cream with Hot Cherries

This is a very old recipe, but not to be overlooked, as it has a good flavour and is quick and easy to do. There are so many mouth-watering ice-creams in the shops now that you will be spoilt for choice, but do choose one with a vanilla base, otherwise you will have too many conflicting tastes.

1 × 400 g / 14 oz tin of black cherries, pitted and drained
2 tbsp Kirsch
450 g / 1 lb vanilla ice-cream

Put the cherries in a saucepan with the Kirsch and slowly heat. Spoon the ice-cream into bowls and, when the cherries are hot, spoon them over the top, then serve immediately.

SERVES 4–6 / 🍶

Butterscotch Sauce

If I behaved myself as a child, I was allowed to have this sauce on vanilla ice-cream. I have to admit that I did not often get the opportunity and probably, for that reason, it is still one of my weaknesses.

125 g / 4 oz golden syrup
125 g / 4 oz soft light-brown sugar
50 g / 2 oz butter
3 tbsp milk
a little vanilla essence

Put the syrup, sugar and butter in a pan, then heat slowly until the sugar dissolves. Gently boil for 1 minute. Add the milk and vanilla essence and boil for 1 more minute. Serve immediately.

SERVES 4 / 🍶

Tantalising Chocolate Sauce

The more you boil the mixture, the stickier it becomes when poured on ice-cream, so if you have an over-talkative guest this could be the best way to sort him or her out. This recipe is unbelievably easy and has a rich, dark chocolate flavour. Serve with bananas, pears and/or ice-cream.

4 dsp golden syrup

4 dsp cocoa powder

Melt the syrup and cocoa powder in a heavy-based saucepan, stirring well. When smooth, dark and about to come to the boil, pour it over the fruit or ice-cream, or leave it to boil, for a sticky texture.

SERVES 4 / ♦

Fruit Brûlé

In this recipe seedless grapes are quick and easy to use, but fresh peach slices, soaked in a little brandy, are also lovely.

450 g | 1 lb seedless grapes, stalks removed

150 ml | 5 fl oz natural yogurt

150 m | 5 fl oz crème fraîche

125 g | 4 oz dark-brown sugar

50 g | 2 oz caster sugar

Put the grapes in a shallow, heatproof serving dish. Mix the yoghurt and crème fraîche in a bowl, then spoon over the grapes. Mix the brown and white sugar together and sprinkle evenly over the top, then put under a preheated hot grill for about 3 minutes or until the sugar is caramelised. Serve hot or chilled.

SERVES 4 / ♦

Fruit Salad

Sadly, it is rare to get a good fruit salad at a large party. Often it is padded out with apples, orange segments with the chewy bits and pith still lurking around the edges, whole grapes full of pips, and soggy bananas. This need not be the case; just use more interesting and/or appropriate fruit in perfect condition, and cut it up small enough to mean that each mouthful contains a variety of fruits and not just one chunk.

1 ripe mango, peeled with a potato peeler and cut into cubes
1 small, ripe pineapple, peeled and cut into cubes
1 small, ripe melon, such as Charentais, peeled, seeded and cut into cubes
1 ripe paw paw, peeled, seeded and cut into cubes
*225 g	8 oz seedless green or black grapes, stalks removed*
*1 × 400 g	14 oz tin of lychees, drained*
juice and pips of 4 passion fruit
4 kiwi fruit, peeled, sliced and halved
3 knobs of stem ginger, cut into tiny cubes
2 tbsp stem ginger syrup

Put all the fruit in a bowl and then mix well. Serve chilled or at room temperature with whipped double cream or crème fraîche.

SERVES 16 / 🖐

Caramelised Clementines

Obviously this can only be cooked in winter but it freezes to perfection. Make sure you buy top-quality, small fruit. They are delicious added to a fruit salad or served with ice-cream or natural yogurt.

*450 g	1 lb clementines, washed*
*450 g	1 lb sugar*

Put the clementines, left whole and unpeeled, the sugar and 600 ml / 1 pint water in a heavy-based saucepan and bring slowly to the boil, stirring occasionally. When the sugar has dissolved turn down the heat to a simmer and cook for about 1 hour, or until a thick syrup forms. Chill and serve.

MAKES 7–8 / 🖐

Paw Paw with Rasperries and Honey

This is a very quick and delicious recipe – but do make sure that the paw paws are in perfect condition. Serve with crème fraîche or whipped cream, if wished. It is also good for breakfast but I would leave out the rum!

2 ripe paw paws, cut into bite-sized pieces
*450 g	1 lb fresh raspberries*
2 tbsp runny honey
2 tbsp dark rum

Mix the ingredients together. Put into serving glasses or bowls and chill for about 2 hours.

SERVES 6 / ❧

Rice Pudding Brûlée with Bay Leaves

I am including this pudding not because it is popular but because the people who do like it are totally addicted. Rice pudding fans, give this a try.

6 tbsp short-grain rice
3 bay leaves
*1.2 l	2 pints milk*
*125 g	4 oz caster sugar*
freshly grated nutmeg
6 dsp sugar

Put the rice in a saucepan, add the bay leaves and milk and gently bring to the boil. Simmer on a very low heat for 25 minutes or until the rice is soft. Add the caster sugar and nutmeg, and stir well. Remove the bay leaves and pour into 6 ramekins. Preheat the grill to a high. Sprinkle the sugar over the top of each ramekin and grill for about 3 minutes or until the tops are bubbling and golden brown. Cool, then chill until ready to serve.

SERVES 6 / ❧

Spiced and Sliced Pears

A beautiful pudding, with its deep red juices and white cream, this is good after a rich main course and quick and easy to prepare. It is an excellent way to use up leftover red wine.

6 firm dessert pears
¼ bottle red wine
*125 g	4 oz soft brown sugar*
rind of 1 lemon
1 stick of cinnamon
*300 ml	10 fl oz double cream, whipped*

Carefully peel the pears, leaving them whole or cutting them into quarters. Remove the cores; if leaving them whole, use a sharp knife to cut out the core but leave the stalk end intact. Place the wine, sugar, rind and cinnamon in a heavy-based pan, then heat gently, stirring. Add the pears, cover and cook over a low heat for 1 hour, turning the pears occasionally. Remove the pears, slice each one $^3/_4$ of the way through into 5–7 slices, place on a serving dish, then gently fan out. Dsicard the cinnamon stick, boil the wine rapidly for a few minutes to make a syrup, then pour over the pears. Chill, then serve with the whipped cream and sweet biscuits of your choice.

SERVES 6 / ♥

Tiramisu

A dish that has been around for years, this has suddenly become fashionable and is now served in many top restaurants. It varies enormously and very few match this one. It is very rich so serve small portions and let the brave come back for seconds.

1 × 125 g / 4 oz packet of boudoir biscuits or Italian sponge cake

6 tsp good instant coffee

450 g / 1 lb Mascarpone cheese

4 egg yolks

125 g / 4 oz caster sugar

1 dsp cocoa powder

Line the bottom of flat serving dish, approximately 20 cm × 30 cm / 8″ × 12″, with biscuits or sponge, cut into fingers. Put 3 tsps instant coffee into a standard (½ pint) mug and pour in boiling water to the top. Stir well, then spoon the coffee over the sponge, soaking it thoroughly. Put the Mascarpone, egg yolks and caster sugar in a bowl and beat until smooth. Pour half the mixture on the biscuits or sponge fingers and smooth with a palette knife. Lay over more biscuits or sponge fingers, fill the mug with the remaining coffee and three-quarters full of boiling water, pour over the pudding, then spread over the remaining cheese mixture. Sift the top heavily with the cocoa powder until the surface is brown, and chill for at least 4 hours before serving.

SERVES 8 /

Lemon Mousse

You can make this lemon mousse without the cream, if wished, especially for serving after a rich main course or for the calorie-conscious. For an extra-light mousse, heat half the lemon juice in a pan and, when beating the egg yolk mixture, add the hot juice. Use the rest of the lemon juice for the gelatine and add a little water, if necessary.

6 eggs, separated
6 tbsp caster sugar
juice and finely grated rind of 2 lemons
1 heaped dsp gelatine
*150 ml	5 fl oz double cream, whipped*
*225 g	8 oz fresh raspberries*
For the decoration:
a little cocoa powder
a few raspberries

Put the egg yolks, sugar and lemon rind in a mixing bowl and beat until thick and creamy. Put the lemon juice in a small saucepan, sprinkle over the gelatine powder, then set aside. Beat the egg whites until stiff. Gently heat the gelatine and fold into the yolk mixture then, using a metal serving spoon, fold in the whipped cream (if you are using it) and egg whites. Mix well, then very carefully fold in 175 g / 6 oz raspberries, stirring as little as possible to prevent the fruit breaking up. Pour into a serving dish and chill. When ready to serve, sieve a little cocoa powder onto the mousse and arrange the remaining raspberries round the edge.

SERVES 6 / 🍷🍷

Strawberries with Zabaglione

For this recipe, you need strawberries with a really full flavour. I have always disliked zabaglione made with Marsala, so after experimenting, I now use whisky, which takes the cloying sweetness out and leaves a velvet texture. (This has always been a closely guarded secret, but I now let the cat out of the bag!) Making zabaglione can be tricky, but if you keep the water just below boiling point to prevent the egg cooking at the edge of the bowl and move the whisk all around the bowl, it should be fine. If you use an electric hand whisk, keep the cable away from the direct heat from the cooker. The zabaglione can be made 1 hour before needed and kept in a thermos to save you having to leave the table for ages after the main course. If you do not have Amaretto, buy a miniature bottle from an off licence or use Grand Marnier or any other sweet liqueur hiding in your cupboard.

350 g | 12 oz strawberries, washed, hulled and quartered
3 tbsp Amaretto
4 egg yolks
4 dsp caster sugar
2 tbsp whisky

Put the strawberries and Amaretto in a bowl and stir thoroughly. Bring to the boil a half-full saucepan of water, then turn down to a low simmer. Put the yolks and sugar in a pudding bowl, stand it in the simmering water and whisk on high for about 3 minutes, then gradually add the whisky. Whisk again for about 2 minutes or until thick, pale and frothy. Remove from the heat and whisk for a minute. (Pour into a preheated thermos, if keeping until later.) Spoon the strawberries into 4 glasses, pour over the zabaglione, then serve immediately.

SERVES 4 / ♠♠

Kinky Pie

Years ago, I worked in a little restaurant in Helford, Cornwall, and learned this recipe for an upside-down apple pie invented by the Munros. It was one of the most popular puddings, so when I moved to London, I brought the recipe with me. It has remained a firm favourite, though I never did find out how it acquired this name.

5 large cooking apples
175 g | 6 oz dark-brown sugar
1 flat dsp ground nutmeg
1 flat dsp ground ginger
2 flat dsp ground cinnamon

| *3 good dsp caster sugar* |
| *225 g | 8 oz shortcrust pastry* |
| *150 ml | 5 fl oz double cream, whipped* |
| *3–4 glacé cherries, halved* |

Preheat the oven to 190°C/375°F/gas mark 5. Using a potato peeler, peel the apples, then using a slicer or a steady hand, slice up the apples at three angles round the core. Cover the base of a 22.5 cm / 9″ baking tin with the brown sugar, pressing down well. Neatly arrange the apple slices over the sugar as this is the top, then continue layering until half the apple is used. Mix the nutmeg, ginger, cinnamon and caster sugar in a bowl and sieve over evenly. Carry on layering until all the apples are used. Roll out the pastry to the size of the tin, wet the edges of the tin, then cover with the pastry. Trim and press the edges down well. Do not worry if the pastry is cracked or untidy, as this is the bottom. Place the tin on a baking tray and bake for about 45 minutes or until it bubbles on the outer edges. Remove from the oven, cool, then when cold, turn out onto a flat serving dish. Cut into 6 or 8 slices, pipe whipped cream onto each slice and decorate with a glacé cherry.

SERVES 6–8 / 🌶🌶 / FREEZE

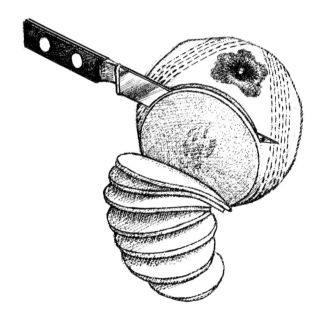

HOW TO CUT THE APPLES

Brown Bread Ice-Cream with Strawberries

An old favourite, and therefore not to be forgotten, this ice-cream requires no stirring during freezing, and you can always have it waiting in the deep freeze. Take ice-cream out of the freezer about 15 minutes before serving to soften slightly.

*35 g	1½ oz butter*
*75 g	3 oz dark-brown sugar*
*125 g	4 oz brown breadcrumbs*
freshly grated nutmeg
*450 ml	15 fl oz double cream*

To serve:

*225 g	8 oz strawberries, washed, hulled and halved*
brandy

Melt the butter in a large frying pan with the sugar, then add the breadcrumbs and nutmeg. Fry over a medium heat for about 8 minutes, stirring frequently until the mixture caramelises. Remove from the heat and cool. Whip the cream to a soft holding consistency. Crumble, then stir in the cold breadcrumb mixture. Pour into a plastic container, cover and freeze until ready to serve. To serve, spoon the ice-cream into bowls, decorate with the prepared strawberries and pour over a splash of brandy.

SERVES 6–8 / 👣👣

Sticky Brownies

This recipe does not lend itself to cooking in large quantities because the outer edges overcook and it is best slightly undercooked, to give the sticky, gooey texture for which it is famous. Microwaves in my view have a limited use but for melting block chocolate they are wonderful – so quick and the chocolate does not stick on the bottom of the pan. Give it a go, if you have one, and you won't look back.

*225 g	8 oz plain chocolate*
*300 g	10 oz dark-brown sugar*
*175 g	6 oz butter*
8 eggs
*225 g	8 oz self-raising flour, sifted*

Preheat the oven to 180°C/350°F/gas mark 4. Line a 17.5 cm × 30 cm / 7″ × 12″ baking tray or roasting tin with greaseproof paper. Melt the chocolate by breaking it up in a bowl and standing the bowl in a pan of simmering water or put into a bowl, add 1 tsp water and put in a microwave on medium heat for 1–2 minutes. Stir with a fork to check that the chocolate has melted. Beat the sugar and butter until fluffy, then gradually beat in the eggs, one at a time. (The mixture may curdle but this does not matter.) Stir in the melted chocolate, then the flour. Pour into the tray or tin, smooth over and bake for about 30 minutes or until the sides are cooked and the middle is still slightly sticky. Cool in the tray or tin, then cut into squares.

MAKES 12–16 PIECES / ♠♠ / FREEZE

Whisked Sponge Cake

A great favourite with slimmers (except for the filling!), this really should be eaten fresh, on the day of cooking, or frozen immediately.

butter for greasing
6 eggs
175 g | 6 oz caster sugar
175 g | 6 oz self-raising flour, sifted
300 ml | 10 fl oz double cream, whipped
225 g | 8 oz strawberries or raspberries, washed, hulled and quartered
a sprinkling of kirsch (optional)
a little icing sugar

Preheat the oven to 180°C/350°F/gas mark 4. Grease and flour a high-sided 20 cm / 8″ cake tin with removable sides. Put the eggs and caster sugar in a large bowl and, preferably using an electric mixer, whisk on high for 5 minutes, or until the mixture is pale and fluffy, and stands in peaks. Whisk again, adding 1 tbsp boiling water. Fold in the flour with a large metal spoon, making sure there are no pockets of flour left in the mixture, then pour into the cake tin. Stand the tin on a baking tray in case it leaks and bake for about 40 minutes or until the top is pale golden. Test by poking a skewer or sharp, thin knife in the centre; it should come out clean. Leave to cool in the tin then, using a long, sharp knife, cut round the edge against the tin and turn out. Cut in half lengthways and fill with the whipped cream, fruit and kirsch. Replace the top and dust with sifted icing sugar.

SERVES 6–8 / ♠♠ / FREEZE (UNFILLED)

Black Treacle Sponge

This recipe dates back to my Scottish grandmother and has been a family favourite ever since, especially with the men. It definitely deserves a sleep afterwards, perhaps after a Sunday lunch.

25 g | 1 oz butter
3 tbsp black treacle
1 tbsp whisky (optional)
125 g | 4 oz self-raising flour
50 g | 2 oz suet
1 tsp powdered ginger
1 tsp baking powder
150 ml | 5 fl oz milk
1 egg
2 tbsp sugar
To serve:
300 ml | 10 fl oz double cream, whipped

Butter a 600 ml / 1 pint pudding basin and put in 1 tablespoon of black treacle and the whisky. Beat the remaining ingredients in a mixing bowl. Pour the mixture into the prepared bowl, cover with greaseproof paper and tie tightly with string or a large elastic band. Put into a large saucepan, half-fill with water and place over the heat. Bring to the boil, reduce the heat and simmer for 1 hour or until cooked but still tacky on top. Check the water level and top up as necessary. Turn out onto a warm plate and serve with lashings of whipped cream.

SERVES 6–8 / 🍶🍶

Flaming Crème Caramels

Every Spanish menu includes these, but oddly enough often translated as 'flan'. I include orange for extra flavour but you can omit it if you prefer. Serve them still warm from the oven, turned out and then flamed in brandy, with fresh raspberries and cream, if wished, or serve chilled without brandy.

For the caramel:
*125 g	4 oz granulated sugar*

For the custard:
*600 ml	20 fl oz milk*
rind of 1 orange, finely grated (optional)
a few drops of vanilla essence
*50 g	2 oz caster sugar*
4 eggs
freshly grated nutmeg
4 tbsp brandy

Preheat the oven to 150°C/300°F/gas mark 2. To make the caramel, put the sugar and 2 tbsp water into a heavy-based saucepan. Heat slowly to dissolve the sugar, then boil rapidly until it turns golden brown. Remove from the heat and, when the bubbles die down, pour into 6 ramekins, coating the bottom of each. Be very careful as caramel is scorching hot. Heat the milk, orange rind, vanilla essence and caster sugar in a saucepan. Beat the eggs in a large bowl. Pour the hot milk into the eggs, whisking continuously. Pour the mixture into the prepared ramekins, then stand them in a baking tin. Pour in sufficient warm water to come ¾ way up the ramekins, then bake for 1 hour or until the custard sets. Remove from the tin, then turn out onto warmed plates. When ready to serve, heat the brandy over a flame, then light it and spoon over each caramel.

SERVES 6 / ♠♠

Lemon and Orange Treacle Tart

Treacle tart is always delicious but with added lemon and orange and lashings of whipped cream, it is outrageously self-indulgent.

For the pastry:
*225 g	8 oz plain flour*
½ tsp salt
*125 g	4 oz butter or margarine*
1 egg yolk

For the filling:
*400 g	14 oz golden syrup*
*350 g	12 oz fine white breadcrumbs*
juice and grated rind of 1 lemon
juice and grated rind of 1 orange

Preheat the oven to 200°C/400°F/gas mark 6. Put the flour and salt in a bowl and rub in the butter or margarine, using fingertips, until it resembles breadcrumbs. Mix in the egg yolk with a round-bladed knife, then gradually add 3 tbsp of water, enough to make the dough stick together. Knead well, then roll out onto a floured surface to about 3 mm / $\frac{1}{8}''$ thick to line a 20 cm / 8″ baking tin. Prick the pastry all over to prevent it rising. To make the filling, put the syrup, straight from the syrup tin, in a saucepan, then warm slightly. Add the remaining ingredients and stir. Put into the pastry case and smooth over. Bake for 30 minutes or until very slightly brown on top. Remove from the oven, allow to cool slightly, then serve with the whipped cream.

SERVES 6–8 / ♨♨ / FREEZE

Meringue Roulade

This recipe was created by accident, but is now a firm favourite. It makes a perfect centrepiece for the buffet table, but remember that you need a large baking tray. Use up the egg yolks by making mayonnaise or my Crème Brûlée (see page 128). The fruit can be varied so choose your own favourites.

6 egg whites
275 g / 10 oz caster sugar
2 tbsp icing sugar, sifted, plus extra for dusting
2 tsp cornflour
a few drops of vinegar
225 g / 8 oz strawberries, hulled and quartered
1 ripe mango, peeled and cut into small cubes
450 ml / 15 fl oz double cream, whipped
50 g / 2 oz grated chocolate (optional)

Preheat the oven to 180°C/350°F/gas mark 4. Line a 45 cm × 30 cm / 18″ × 12″ baking tray with greaseproof paper. Whisk the egg whites until stiff. Continue whisking fast, then add the caster sugar a spoonful at a time. The mixture should be thick and white. Using a serving spoon, fold in the icing sugar and cornflour and add the vinegar. Put into the baking tray, smooth and bake for 30 minutes or until set on the top but still soft in the middle. Cool. Mix the strawberries and mango in a bowl. Turn the meringue out upside down onto a fresh greaseproof paper, then spread with whipped cream. Arrange the fruit evenly on the top and sprinkle with the grated chocolate, if using. Holding the long ends, roll up fairly tightly like a Swiss Roll and then, using both hands, lift onto a flat serving dish. Flurry with icing sugar, chill and serve, cut in slices like a Swiss Roll.

SERVES 8–10 / 🍒

Chestnut Meringue Cake

If you want an unusual birthday cake to round off a dinner party, this is it. One of our most popular puddings, it works any time of year. An alternative filling is whipped cream with red fruit.

8 egg whites
*450 g	1 lb caster sugar*
*1 × 400 g	14 oz tin of unsweetened chestnut purée*
*75 g	3 oz dark plain chocolate, melted in 1 tbsp water*
*75 g	3 oz dark-brown sugar*
*300 ml	10 fl oz double cream, whipped*
icing sugar

Preheat the oven to 180°C/350°F/gas mark 4. Whisk the egg whites until stiff and then add the caster sugar, still whisking on high, one spoon at a time. Put into 2 × 30 cm / 12″ round baking tins lined with greaseproof paper and smooth over. Bake for 20 minutes or until the meringue is very lightly brown. Cool. Beat the chestnut purée, melted chocolate and brown sugar in a bowl and, when smooth, fold in the whipped cream. Remove the meringue from the tins and peel off the paper. (If the paper sticks, wet it with a soaking cloth, wait 1 minute, then peel off.) Place a meringue layer on a serving dish, then spread over the chestnut filling. Top with the other meringue layer and flurry over a little icing sugar. Serve chilled.

SERVES 8–10 / ❦❦ / FREEZE

Chestnut Syllabub

This makes a very good winter pudding served in a glass and decorated with grated chocolate. The mixture can also be used in our Meringue Roulade (see page 113) or Chestnut Meringue Cake (see above). Surprisingly, it freezes well in a meringue roulade or cake.

*1 × 175 g	6 oz tin of unsweetened chestnut purée*
1 tbsp dark-brown sugar
1 tbsp brandy
*225 ml	8 fl oz double cream*
*25 g	1 oz dark chocolate, grated*

Put the chestnut purée in a bowl with the brown sugar and brandy, then whisk until smooth. Add the double cream and whisk again. When light and smooth, spoon into 4 glasses and sprinkle with the grated chocolate. Serve chilled.

SERVES 4 / ❦❦

Pears in Hazelnut Pastry

For this recipe, you must use soft, ripe, eating pears, but you will find it well worth waiting for the right time of year. If you do not have pear liqueur you could use an orange liqueur such as Cointreau instead. Whipped cream is a very important part of this pudding!

*125 g	4 oz plain flour*
*50 g	2 oz ground hazelnuts*
1 tsp caster sugar
*75 g	3 oz butter*
8 medium-sized ripe pears
8 dsp pear liqueur
*300 ml	10 fl oz double cream, whipped*

Preheat the oven to 190°C/375°F//gas mark 5. Mix the flour, nuts and sugar in a bowl. Rub in the butter with your fingertips until the mixture resembles breadcrumbs, then, using a round-bladed knife, stir in enough water to hold the dough together. Knead with your hand, then turn out onto a floured board. Alternatively, make the pastry in a blender. Roll out to 6 mm / ¼″ thick, then cut into 8 rounds and place in small-cup baking tins, as for making mince pies. Press down well and bake for about 15 minutes or until golden. Use the remaining pastry to make leaf shapes as decorations. Remove from the tins and cool. Peel the pears, leaving them whole, core from beneath, then cut the bottoms flat, so they stand securely. Place a pear in each pastry cup, on individual serving plates, pour a spoonful of liqueur over each, decorate with pastry leaves and serve with a bowl of whipped cream.

SERVES 8 / ♦♦

Jack Hawkins' Cheesecake

There are now so many variations on cheesecakes but twenty years ago cheesecake was virtually unheard of in England. Jack and his wife Doreen Hawkins went to America to work on a film, and when they returned they gave me this pudding that contained cheese, of all things! It turned out to be delicious, and although the dish is now very well known, I have never tasted any cheesecake recipe to beat this one.

1 × 200 g / 7 oz packet of ginger biscuits
125 g / 4 oz butter
250 g / 9 oz cream cheese
200 g / 7 oz caster sugar
½ tsp vanilla essence
2 eggs

For the topping:
300 ml / 10 fl oz soured cream
½ tsp vanilla essence
1 dsp caster sugar

Crush the biscuits by putting them in a plastic bag and stabbing them with the end of a rolling pin, or breaking them up and putting them in a blender. Melt the butter, mix in the crumbs, then line the base of a shallow 20 cm / 8″ cake tin, pressing down evenly and firmly. Beat the cream cheese, sugar and vanilla essence until smooth, then add the eggs and beat well. Pour onto the biscuit base, then put in a cold oven set to 180°C/350°F/gas mark 4. Bake for about 40 minutes or until the mixture is just set but not brown. Mix together in a bowl the soured cream, vanilla essence and sugar, then spoon and smooth over the top of the hot pie. Put back in the oven for 3 minutes, then remove and chill. Cut the slices directly from the baking tin and arrange on a serving dish.

SERVES 8 / ●● / FREEZE

Praline Soufflé

An unusual soufflé made with coffee and nutty caramel pieces, this is good served with Fruit Salad (see page 98). The caramel can be made in advance and kept in an airtight tin for a few days, but make the soufflé the day it is to be served, as the caramel can turn runny overnight.

2 tbsp sugar
a little vegetable oil
*25 g	1 oz mixed nuts, finely chopped and browned*
3 eggs, separated
3 dsp caster sugar
3 tsp instant coffee powder
2 level tsp gelatine
*150 ml	5 fl oz double cream, whipped*

To make the praline, first oil a baking sheet. Place the sugar in a heavy-based saucepan with 2 tbsp water. Place over a low heat to dissolve the sugar, then turn the heat up and boil rapidly until the syrup turns golden brown. Remove from the heat, let the bubbles die down, then add the chopped nuts. Stir well, then pour onto the oiled sheet. The mixture is scalding hot, so be careful. Spread out and leave to cool. When cool and crisp, break up, place in a bowl and crush with the end of a rolling pin – or use a blender – until it resembles small crunchy crumbs.

To make the soufflé, put the egg yolks and caster sugar in a bowl and whisk hard. Pour 2 tbsp boiling water over the coffee in a cup and, when dissolved, pour into the egg-yolk mixture. Whisk again until light brown and fluffy. The heat of the water will help fluff up the mixture. Put 1 tbsp cold water in a small saucepan, sprinkle over the gelatine, leave for 1 minute and then put over a very low heat until dissolved and transparent. Add to the coffee mixture and stir well. Fold in the whipped cream and praline crumbs. Immediately, whisk the egg whites until stiff, then fold in, using a large metal spoon. Pour into a soufflé dish and leave to set. Sprinkle over a little instant coffee powder and serve.

SERVES 4 🌢🌢

Strawberry Syllabub Trifle

This is a change from the usual trifle and has a lovely summery feel, although as you can buy strawberries all year round, it is a delightful winter treat as well.

4 tbsp Amaretto
4 tbsp sherry
*1 × 450 g	1 lb bought lemon sponge cake*
*450 g	1 lb strawberries, hulled and halved, plus extra for decoration*
*1 × 400 g	14 oz tin of ready-made custard*
*300 ml	10 fl oz double cream*
juice and rind of 1 lemon
2 tbsp icing sugar, sifted
4 tbsp white wine
1 tbsp brandy

Mix the Amaretto and sherry in a jug. Break the cake into small pieces and lay a few on the bottom of a 1.2 litre / 2 pint soufflé dish. Sprinkle with alcohol, then cover with a layer of strawberries. Repeat until all the ingredients are used. Pour over the custard and smooth. Whip the double cream until quite stiff, then add the lemon juice and rind, icing sugar, white wine and brandy. Whisk again until the mixture is smooth and stiff. Pour over the top of the trifle, smooth over and decorate with the strawberries. Chill until ready to serve.

SERVES 6–8 / 🍶🍶

Black Forest Roulade

Who could say 'no' to this chocolate roulade, with its cherries drowned in Kirsch and whipped cream? When in season, use fresh black cherries but remember to remove the stones and cut each cherry into quarters to make rolling it up easy.

5 eggs, separated
*150 g	5 oz caster sugar*
*150 g	5 oz plain block chocolate*
*1 × 400 g	14 oz tin of black cherries, pitted and drained*
1 tbsp Kirsch
*300 ml	10 fl oz double cream, whipped*
icing sugar

Preheat the oven to 180°C/350°F/gas mark 4. Line a 20 cm × 27.5 cm / 8″ × 11″ baking tray with greaseproof paper. Beat the egg yolks and caster sugar until light and fluffy. Put the chocolate and 1 tbsp water into a small saucepan and either stand it in boiling water or put it over a very low heat until the chocolate melts. Whisk the egg whites until stiff. Stir the melted chocolate into the egg-yolk mixture, then fold in the egg whites until the mixture is smooth. Pour into the prepared baking tray and bake for about 10 minutes or until just set. Remove and leave to cool. Put the cherries in a bowl with the Kirsch and mix well. Turn out the roulade onto a clean cloth dusted with icing sugar, spread with the whipped cream right to the edges, then lay over the cherries, again right to the edges. Roll the roulade up, holding the long edges, then flurry with icing sugar. Lift onto a serving plate and chill until ready to serve.

SERVES 6 / ♦♦

Grand Marnier Soufflés

Years ago, my great hero, Anton Mosimann, gave me the idea for this soufflé, with its delicious pool of liqueur on the top, and I still cannot come up with a better way, damn it! The only nuisance is preparing each ramekin but once this is done, the rest is fairly quick. A small melon baller is essential, otherwise the decoration is not possible.

12 large eggs, separated
*350 g	12 oz caster sugar*
rind and juice of 1½ large oranges
2 heaped tsp gelatine
1 tbsp Grand Marnier
*300 ml	10 fl oz double cream, whipped*

For the decoration:
a little cocoa powder
8 tsp Grand Marnier
8 sprigs of dill or chervil

Measure the height of the ramekins. Cut 4 bands of double thickness greaseproof paper, each 2.5 cm / 1″ higher than the ramekins. Wrap a band of paper round each ramekin and hold in place with string, elastic bands or sticky tape, whichever way you find easiest. Make sure the band is taut round the top of each ramekin. Put the egg yolks, sugar and rind in a bowl and whisk over a bowl of hot water until the mixture is light and fluffy. Pour the orange juice in a small saucepan and sprinkle over the gelatine. Leave to soak for

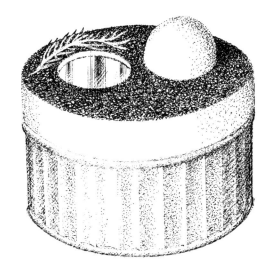

HOW TO GARNISH

1 minute. Whisk the egg whites until stiff. Heat the gelatine mixture very slowly and when transparent and the gelatine has dissolved, stir into the egg-yolk mixture. Swiftly fold in the Grand Marnier, whipped cream and, finally, the egg whites. Spoon into the prepared ramekins, taking the mixture up to the top of the paper, then smooth over. Chill until set. Remove the papers very carefully. Sift a little cocoa powder over the top of each soufflé, using a tea strainer or fine sieve. Heat a small melon baller in a cup of hot water, dry it, then scoop out a ball from each soufflé, putting the ball upside down on the soufflé beside the hole. Pour a teaspoon of Grand Marnier into each hole, decorate with herbs, then serve.

SERVES 8 / ♠♠♠ / FREEZE

Crêpes Suzette

This is one of the best-known French puddings, and no wonder – it's fun to make and full of delicious flavours. A vicar friend of mine once went slightly out of control when lighting the alcohol and nearly sent his cassock up in flames, so take care! The pancakes can be made in advance and even frozen.

8 Pancakes (see page 54 and omit the parsley and Tabasco)
25 g / 1 oz unsalted butter
50 g / 2 oz caster sugar
finely grated rind and juice of 1 large orange
juice of ½ lemon
a good splash of Grand Marnier

Heat the butter and sugar in a large, heavy-based frying pan and when slightly caramelised, add the orange rind and juices. When bubbling, reduce the heat a little and place in a pancake, fold in half with a palette knife, then in half again. Move to one side of the pan, then repeat with the remaining pancakes. Pour in the Grand Marnier, turn up the heat and set alight. When the flames die down, place 2 pancakes each on warmed, individual plates, then serve immediately.

SERVES 4 / ♠♠♠

Lemon or Lime Meringue Pie

This is, without doubt, the best meringue pie I have ever tasted. The almonds in the pastry give an extra flavour and the extra butter and no water make it deliciously crumbly, which is why I do not roll it out. Adding beaten egg white to the lemon filling makes it light and fluffy, far removed from the usual heavy jelly-like texture. It is not terribly easy to make, so practise for consumption by close friends or family first. It can be frozen.

For the pastry:
125 g	4 oz butter, softened
2 dsp caster sugar
125 g	4 oz plain flour
50 g	2 oz ground almonds

For the filling:
1 heaped dsp cornflour
300 ml	10 fl oz milk
3 heaped dsp sugar
grated rind and juice of 1 large lemon or 2 limes
5 eggs, separated
8 heaped dsp caster sugar

Preheat the oven to 190°C/375°F/gas mark 5. To make the pastry, rub the butter into the mixed dry ingredients or put everything in a blender and blend until the pastry forms a ball. Press out with your fingertips into a 20 cm / 8″ flan ring, dusting the pastry with a little flour to prevent your fingers sticking to the pastry and making sure to bring the pastry evenly up the sides. Prick the base with a fork and bake for about 25 minutes or until golden brown. Remove from the oven. Turn the oven temperature down to 150°C/ 300°F/gas mark 2.

To make the filling, put the cornflour and a little of the milk in a cup and blend to a smooth liquid. Heat the remaining milk in a heavy-based saucepan with the lemon rind and when it starts to simmer, remove it from the heat. Add the cornflour mixture, stirring continuously with a whisk, then return it to a low heat until thick. Stir in the sugar and lemon or lime juice, remove from the heat, then stir in the egg yolks. Whisk the egg whites until stiff in a clean. dry bowl, remove 1 dessertspoonful and fold into the lemon or lime mixture. Gradually add half the caster sugar to the egg whites, whisking continuously until creamy and thick. Fold in the rest of the caster sugar. Pour the lemon or lime mixture into the cooked pastry case and smooth over. Spoon the meringue very gently over the top of the pie, starting from the edge and working inwards. (If the lemon or lime mixture is too runny, put the pie without the meringue into the oven for 10 minutes.) Bake for 30–45 minutes or until the meringue is firm but not brown. Serve warm or cold.

SERVES 6 / ●●● / FREEZE

Lemon and Lime Roulade with Raspberries

The sponge in this recipe is fragile but, to avoid last-minute tension, it can be prepared in advance and frozen, whole or in slices (a useful stand-by for the unexpected guest, as a slice will thaw in minutes).

*225 g	8 oz cream cheese*
8 eggs, separated
rind of 2 lemons, juice of 1 lemon
rind and juice of 1 lime
10 dsp caster sugar
*450 ml	15 fl oz double cream, whipped*
*225 g	8 oz fresh raspberries*
icing sugar

Preheat the oven to 170°C/325°F/gas mark 3. Line a 38 cm × 25 cm / 15″ × 10″ baking tin with greaseproof paper. Whisk the cream cheese, egg yolks, lemon and lime rind and sugar together until light and fluffy. Add the fruit juices and stir. Whisk the egg whites and fold into the mixture. Pour into the prepared tin and bake for 20 minutes or until set but not brown. Leave to cool. Turn out onto fresh greaseproof paper dusted with icing sugar, then carefully peel off the old paper. Spread the sponge with the whipped cream and distribute the raspberries evenly on the top. Holding the corners of the long ends, carefully roll up, using the paper to help you. Carefully lift the roulade onto a serving dish, dust with icing sugar and chill. Serve by cutting like a Swiss Roll.

SERVES 8 / ●●● / FREEZE

Floating Islands

This is an all-time favourite of mine; I have eaten it in many restaurants, but I seldom seem to remember to make it myself. There are numerous versions of this classic French recipe, îles flottantes, but this one with caramel and almonds is, to me, the best. It can be made 4–5 hours in advance and put together at the last minute. If the custard curdles, immediately transfer it to a liquidiser and blend on high speed.

8 eggs, separated
*350 g	12 oz caster sugar*
*1.2 litres	2 pints of milk*
a few drops of vanilla essence
For the caramel sauce:
*125 g	4 oz golden syrup*
*125 g	4 oz soft light-brown sugar*
*50 g	2 oz butter*
3 tbsp milk
2 tbsp flaked almonds, browned

To make the 'islands', whisk the egg whites until stiff, then whisk in 225 g / 8 oz caster sugar. Heat the milk in a large saucepan and, when near boiling, reduce the heat to low and, using a serving spoon, spoon in 2 large dollops of raw meringue. Baste with the milk for about 3 minutes, remove each 'island' with a slotted spoon, then place on a tray. Repeat, cooking the other 4 meringues.

To make the custard, whisk the egg yolks and the remaining caster sugar in a bowl until thick. Bring the milk back to the boil, pour over the egg yolk mixture, then add the vanilla essence. Pour back into the saucepan and, being careful not to let it boil, stir continuously over a low heat until the custard thickens. When it coats the back of a spoon, remove from the heat, cool slightly, then place a layer of clingfilm over the top to prevent a skin forming. Chill.

To make the caramel sauce, put the syrup, brown sugar and butter into a saucepan, then heat gently to dissolve. Add the milk and then boil gently for 1 minute. To serve, divide the custard between 6 bowls. Place a meringue 'island' in each bowl, then pour warm caramel in zig-zag lines over the custard and meringues. Sprinkle with flaked almonds, then serve.

SERVES 6 / ♦♦♦

Praline Profiteroles

This makes a good change from the usual profiteroles with chocolate sauce. The choux balls can be made in advance and frozen; I make double quantities and keep the other half for another day.

For the pastry:
*75 g	3 oz plain flour*
a pinch of salt
*150 ml	5 fl oz half water and half milk*
*50 g	2 oz butter*
2 large eggs

For the praline cream:
a little vegetable oil
2 tbsp sugar
*25 g	1 oz mixed nuts, finely chopped*
*300 ml	10 fl oz double cream, whipped*
1 tbsp brandy

Preheat the oven to 220°C/425°F/gas mark 7. Put the flour and salt in a small bowl. Put the water, milk and butter in a saucepan and heat gently until the butter melts, then bring to a rapid boil and quickly tip the flour and salt into the bubbling liquid. Beat hard with a wooden spoon until the mixture is smooth, leave the sides of the pan and has a sheen. Beat the eggs in, one at a time, and then beat until the mixture is smooth. Using 2 teaspoons, scoop out portions the size of the teaspoon. Place on a greased baking tray, leaving 5 cm / 2″ between each choux ball, to allow for expansion. Cook for about 15 minutes or until each ball is well risen and crisp on the outside. Cool slightly, then cut halfway through each one. (Freeze them at this point, if you want.)

While the choux balls are cooking you can make the praline. Oil a baking sheet. Place the sugar in a heavy-based saucepan with 2 tbsp water. Place over a low heat to dissolve the sugar, then turn the heat up and boil rapidly until the syrup turns golden brown. Remove from the heat, let the bubbles die down, then add the chopped nuts. Stir well, then pour onto the oiled sheet. The mixture is scalding hot, so be careful. Spread out and leave to cool. When cool and crisp, break up, place in a bowl and crush with the end of a rolling pin – or use a blender – until it resembles small crunchy crumbs. Fold into the whipped cream, then add the brandy. Open the cut choux balls in your hand and, using a teaspoon, fill each one and then close. Pile on a plate, then chill until ready to serve.

MAKES 25–30 (SERVES 5–6) / ♦♦♦

Crème Brûlée

Fattening? Well, yes, but you can't be good all the time. Many people shy away from making this recipe but here is a very safe way. Make sure to have a very hot grill. I often put a dessertspoon of cooked blackcurrants or sliced Spiced and Sliced Pears (see page 103) in the bottom of the ramekin as a surprise under the crispy top. You can freeze the egg whites in an airtight container or make an irresistible Meringue Roulade (see page 113).

6 egg yolks
450 ml / 15 fl oz double cream
1 flat dsp caster sugar
a few drops of vanilla essence
2 dsp soft brown sugar
2 dsp caster sugar

Beat the egg yolks in a large, heatproof bowl. Put the cream, caster sugar and vanilla essence in a heavy-based saucepan. Heat, stirring gently with a whisk, to boiling point. When about to boil, pour the cream mixture over the egg yolks, whisking continuously as you pour. Pour the mixture into individual ramekins. If the cream is hot enough, the custard should set without further cooking; test by coating the back of a spoon. If the mixture is not coating the spoon, place the ramekins in an ovenproof tin, half filled with warm water, and place in an oven heated to 180°C/350°F/gas mark 4 for about 30 minutes or until just set. Cool, then refrigerate. Preheat the grill to very hot. Cover the top of each custard with a mixture of soft brown sugar and caster sugar, smooth over and place under grill for about 3 minutes. Watch all the time and remove as soon as the sugar caramelises and bubbles. Use good oven gloves as the ramekins are very hot. Leave to cool, then refrigerate and serve cold.

SERVES 4 / ♦♦♦

Stilton and Broccoli Flan (page 132).

Spinach and Egg Mayonnaise Roulade (page 135) and Prawn and Almond Roulade (page 140).

Salmon Platter (page 138).

Caesar Salad (page 143).

Grilled Mixed Vegetables (page 141).

Tomato and Mozzarella Salad (page 145).

Carrot and Orange Salad (page 146).

Cucumber and Strawberry Salad (page 146).

Irish Coffee

Instead of using whisky, you can use vodka for Russian coffee, Kahlua and call it Mexican coffee or make your own up by browsing in your drinks cupboard. Adding sugar to the coffee and letting the tip of a warmed spoon touch the coffee helps keep the cream floating on top. Also, make sure the coffee is still when pouring in the cream. It's a lovely, glamorous end to a good meal.

600 ml / 1 pint freshly made, strong, black coffee (hot)
4 small tsp sugar
4 tbsp whisky
150 ml / 5 fl oz double cream

Put a teaspoon of sugar in each of 4 glasses. Pour coffee in each glass, leaving a 2.5 cm / 1" space at the top. Pour the whisky in each glass and stir well. Place the tip of a warmed spoon into the top of each coffee and pour a quarter of the cream slowly over the back of the spoon. Remove the spoon and repeat with the other glasses.

SERVES 4 / 🍶🍶

Buffet Parties

If you have a lot of invitations to get off your chest, so to speak, a buffet party is a very good way to repay hospitality. It is less fiddly than a cocktail party, although you do have more washing up at the end. Buffet parties tend to produce more serious conversations, as everyone stays put in one place for longer, and this is often more satisfying for the guests. All the cooking can be done in advance and the food can even be put out on a table just before the guests arrive, if you are using two rooms for entertaining. I think it is a good touch to produce at least one hot item in the meal; one obvious choice is Herb and Garlic Bread (see page 151), which goes down a treat – if you have a large party and a queue forming for food, have someone walk down the queue with the bread as a peace offering for the wait.

It is important to get the balance of food right. In the summer I choose one fish, one meat and one vegetarian dish, and three different salads with varying textures: one green and crisp, one colourful and fresh, such as Carrot and Orange Salad (see page 146), and one filling, such as Brown Rice Salad (see page 148). In the winter I replace cold meats with a casserole or cassoulet or even brave a Paella, but still serve salads. (Recipes for these main courses are from the previous chapter, and quantities may need to be increased; the same applies to puddings.) This way there is plenty of variety and everybody should be happy. Make sure that all the food is cut up small so that it is easy to eat standing up or perched on a chair. I always choose one 'naughty' pudding, such as Black Forest Roulade (see page 119), and one 'good' one, such as our special Fruit Salad (see page 98); greedy guests can have both and the excuse is that they go beautifully together. I also provide a small cheese board for those who don't eat puddings; there are always a few, and this touch ends off the meal well. Though a nuisance, it is also good to serve coffee; a useful tip is to make some real coffee before the guests arrive and keep it in thermoses.

MEAT, FISH AND VEGETABLE DISHES

Pissaladière

A cross between a quiche and a pizza, this is good served hot or cold.

For the pastry:
175 g / 6 oz plain flour
75 g / 3 oz butter
25 g / 1 oz Parmesan, finely grated
1 tsp chopped organo
¼ tsp salt

For the filling:
a little olive oil
2 × 50 g / 1.76 oz tins of anchovies
1 onion, peeled and finely chopped
1 garlic clove, peeled and crushed
1 × 400 g / 14 oz tin of chopped tomatoes
1 dsp tomato purée
salt and freshly ground black pepper
1 tsp dried mixed herbs
2 dsp black olive paste
25 g / 1 oz Parmesan, finely grated
25 g / 1 oz pitted black olives, halved

Preheat the oven to 200°C/400°F/gas mark 6. Whizz all the dry pastry ingredients in a blender, gradually adding a little water until the mixture forms a dough ball. Remove and knead lightly on a floured surface. Roll out, then line a 22.5 cm / 9″ quiche dish. Trim the edges and bake for 10 minutes. Check and pat the pastry down if it has risen, then cook for a further 10 minutes or until lightly golden. Heat the olive oil and anchovy oil in a frying pan, add the onion and garlic and gently cook for 10 minutes or until the onion is soft but not brown. Add the tomatoes, tomato purée, salt, pepper and herbs. Simmer for 15 minutes, or until it thickens. Spread the black olive paste on the cooked pastry, then pour in the tomato mixture. Sprinkle over the Parmesan, lay the anchovy fillets in crosses and decorate with the black olives. Cook for a further 15 minutes, then serve hot or cold.

SERVES 6–8 / 🥄

Stilton and Broccoli Flan

Serve this tasty alternative to ordinary quiche slightly warm.

*75 g	3 oz butter*
*175 g	6 oz plain flour*
1 small handful of parsley, stalks removed
salt and freshly ground black pepper

For the filling:

*450 g	1 lb broccoli florets, blanched in salted water*
*25 g	1 oz margarine*
1 onion, peeled and finely chopped
*25 g	1 oz flour*
*200 ml	7 fl oz milk*
*125 g	4 oz Stilton cheese, rind removed*
*25 g	1 oz cheddar cheese*
paprika

Preheat the oven to 200°C/400°F/gas mark 6. Put the butter, flour, parsley and salt into a blender and blend until the mixture resembles breadcrumbs, then add a little cold water and continue blending until the mixture forms a dough ball. Remove and knead on a floured surface. Roll out to 6 mm / ¼″ thick, then line a 22.5 cm / 9″ quiche dish. Bake for 10 minutes, remove and press down the pastry if it has risen, then return to the oven for 10 minutes or until cooked but not brown. Melt the margarine in a saucepan, sauté the onion for 10 minutes or until soft but not brown, then stir in the flour. Add the milk, stirring continuously to make a smooth sauce. Grind in some fresh pepper. Crumble in the Stilton. Place the broccoli in the cooked pastry case, stir sauce and then pour over broccoli, sprinkle over the cheddar cheese and paprika and bake for 30 minutes or until lightly brown.

SERVES 6–8 / 🍶🍶

Tartlet Cases with Onion and Basil

These are excellent for a buffet table. The cases can be made up to a week in advance and the filling can be made a day in advance, but spoon the mixture into the cases at the last minute to keep the pastry crisp.

For the pastry:

*175 g	6 oz plain flour*
salt
*75 g	3 oz butter*
1 tsp black olive paste

For the filling:

2 tbsp olive oil
4 onions, peeled and finely chopped
1 handful of fresh basil, finely chopped
salt and freshly ground black pepper
a pinch of sugar (optional)

For the garnish:

10 asparagus spears, blanched and halved lengthways

Preheat the oven to 200°C/400°F/gas mark 6. Blend the flour, salt, butter and olive paste in a blender. Add a little water gradually until the mixture forms a dough ball. Remove and knead lightly on a floured surface. Roll out and line mince pie-sized baking tins. Bake for 15 minutes or until cooked and light brown. Leave to cool slightly, then remove from the tins. Put all the filling ingredients in a frying pan and fry gently for 10 minutes or until the onion is very soft but not brown. Test for seasoning then leave to cool. When ready to serve, spoon the mixture into each pastry shell, garnish with a halved asparagus spear, then arrange on a serving dish.

MAKES 20 / 🍶🍶

Coulibiac

This is equally good served hot, or cold at a buffet table. It is normally served with soured cream but recently we cooked it for Gayle Hunnicutt and she suggested a tomato and basil sauce which was delicious. When you roll out the pastry, make sure that it will sit into a baking tray that will fit into your oven.

75 g / 3 oz butter
1 onion, peeled and finely chopped
225 g / 8 oz flat mushrooms, wiped and sliced
450 g / 1 lb salmon fillet, skinned
150 ml / 5 fl oz white wine
salt and freshly ground black pepper
225 g / 8 oz white rice
4 hard-boiled eggs, peeled and chopped
450 g / 1 lb shortcrust pastry
150 ml / 5 fl oz soured cream
1 egg, beaten
1 tbsp milk

To accompany:

300 ml / 10 fl oz soured cream or Tomato and Basil Sauce (see page 68)

Preheat the oven to 200°C/400°F/gas mark 6. Put the butter and onion in a frying pan and cook on a low heat for 8 minutes or until the onion is soft. Add the mushrooms and cook for a further 5 minutes. Put the salmon in an ovenproof dish with the white wine and seasoning. Cover and bake for 15 minutes or until cooked. Pour the white wine into a large saucepan, then add the rice. Add 150 ml / 5 fl oz water, bring to the boil, reduce the heat and simmer for 10 minutes or until the rice is cooked and the liquid, absorbed. Top up with water if necessary. Flake the salmon flesh when cool. Add the mushroom mixture, salmon and hard-boiled eggs to the rice. Stir well and season again. Roll out the pastry to form a rectangle the size of a baking tray that fits your oven. Spoon the mixture down the centre of the pastry, roll up pastry and press well along the join. Turn over so that the pastry join is underneath. Seal the ends tightly. Mix the beaten egg with the milk, then brush over the pastry. Decorate with pastry shapes, such as little fish, from the leftover pastry, then brush with the egg wash. Place on a baking tray lined with greaseproof paper, then bake for 30 minutes or until the pastry is golden brown. Serve warm or chilled with either sauce.

SERVES 6–8 / ❦❦ / FREEZE

Smoked Mackerel Roulade with Gooseberries

A roulade on a buffet table makes a pleasant change from quiche. This smoked mackerel roulade is particularly good, but the possibilities are endless; alternative recipes are given below and overleaf.

225 g | 8 oz smoked mackerel fillet
5 eggs, separated
freshly ground black pepper

For the filling:
350 g | 12 oz cream cheese
225 g | 8 oz gooseberries, frozen and defrosted or tinned (drained)

Preheat the oven to 180°C/350°F/gas mark 4. Line a baking tray 35 cm × 27.5 cm / 14″ × 11″ with greaseproof paper. Blend the smoked mackerel with the egg yolks and pepper until fairly smooth. Whisk the egg whites until stiff, then fold into the mackerel mixture. Pour into the baking tray, smooth over right into the corners, then bake for 15 minutes or until set but not brown. Leave to cool. Mix the cream cheese and gooseberries. Turn out the mackerel mixture onto a clean tea towel, spread over the gooseberry mixture to the corners, then roll up, holding the 2 longer edges. Wrap in the cloth to secure and leave until ready to serve. Unwrap and cut into slices like a Swiss Roll.

SERVES 8 / 👢👢

Spinach and Egg Mayonnaise Roulade

225 g | 8 oz cooked spinach, chopped
5 eggs, separated
freshly ground nutmeg, to taste
salt and freshly ground black pepper

For the filling:
6 eggs, hard boiled, peeled and chopped finely
5 tbsp Mayonnaise (see page 154)
salt and freshly ground black pepper

Follow the previous recipe but use spinach instead of smoked mackerel. Mix the ingredients for the filling together and follow the recipe instructions as before.

Sprout and Chestnut Roulade

225 g	8 oz Brussels sprouts, cooked and puréed
5 eggs, separated
salt and freshly ground black pepper

For the filling:
175 g	6 oz tin of chestnut purée
125 g	4 oz cream cheese
salt and freshly ground black pepper

Follow the two preceding recipes, but blend the filling to a smooth consistency.

Chicken Carabela

As a family we invented this recipe many years ago. It was christened Carabela because my sister is called Carole and my parents and close friends call me Clara Belle or Belle so the recipe combines each name. I started using it professionally in 1973 and it is still the most popular cold dish that I serve. You can make double quantity, or more, of the sauce and freeze it in portions at the stage before adding the mayonnaise.

1 × 1.4 kilo	3 lb chicken, cooked and the meat cut into bite-sized cubes, and the carcass reserved
1 tbsp oil
1 small onion, peeled and finely chopped
2 tsp mild curry powder
1 tbsp tomato purée
juice of 1 lemon
75 ml	3 fl oz chicken stock or water
2 heaped tbsp sweet mango chutney
300 ml	10 fl oz Mayonnaise (see page 154)
1 ripe mango or 125 g	4 oz seedless grapes

Boil the chicken carcass for about 30 minutes in 600 ml / 1 pint water to make the stock, or, since the sauce has a strong flavour anyway, just use water. Put the oil, onion and curry powder in a frying pan and fry slowly for 10 minutes or until soft. Add the stock or water, tomato purée, lemon juice and chutney. Stir well and simmer for 5 minutes. Leave to cool. Stir in the mayonnaise, then add the chicken. Transfer to a serving dish, then garnish with slices of peeled ripe mango or seedless grapes.

SERVES 4–6 / 🐦🐦

Cornish Pasties

As a lover of Cornwall and the Cornish, I can't let this book go by without including this recipe. It reputedly got its name because, as the tin miners' lunch was thrown down the shaft, their wives shouted, 'Look what's coming past 'ee!' It's a good yarn, anyway. Home-made pasties are still a great lunch and are well worth the effort. Originally they had meat at one end and apple or jam at the other, to make a complete lunch in one, but I have left out the sweet end. They can be frozen after cooking but are best eaten fresh from the oven.

1.35 kg | 3 lb shortcrust pastry (see French Mushroom Tartlets recipe on page 56 and quadruple the quantities)

*225–300 g	8–10 oz of potatoes, peeled and very thinly sliced or diced for easy handling*
1 onion, peeled and finely diced
*350 g	12 oz swede, peeled and finely diced*
*450 g	1 lb chuck steak or skirt, diced or minced*
salt and freshly ground black pepper
1 tbsp mixed herbs
1 egg, beaten
1 dsp milk

Preheat the oven to 200°C/400°F/gas mark 6. Roll the pastry out to 6 mm | ¼″ thick, then cut 12 rounds, using a 17.5 cm | 7″ plate as a template. Mix the remaining ingredients, except the egg and milk, in a large bowl, then divide into 12 and place down the centre of each pastry circle. Wet the edges of the pastry with water, then fold over and join the 2 edges, pressing firmly to seal and make a crimped effect. Mix the egg and milk in a cup then brush the pasty. Place on a baking tray and bake for 20 minutes. Reduce the heat to 160°C/325°F/gas mark 3 for a further 25 minutes. Serve hot.

MAKES 12 | ♦♦ | FREEZE

Salmon Platter

This dish looks particularly attractive on a buffet table, suits most tastes and makes a change from whole dressed salmon. You can also use crab meat instead of salmon. St André cheese can be bought in most supermarkets, but use Brie if hard to find.

12 quail eggs
900 g | 2 lb salmon fillet, cooked
salt and freshly ground black pepper
225 g | 8 oz mange tout, topped and tailed
225 g | 8 oz French beans, topped and tailed
225 g | 8 oz oyster mushrooms
2 tbsp olive oil
1 curly endive, washed
225 g | 8 oz St André cheese, or similar, cut into 2.5 cm | 1" cubes
225 g | 8 oz cherry tomatoes, stalks removed
125 g | 4 oz pine nuts (optional)
150 ml | 5 fl oz French Dressing (see page 153)

Put the quail eggs in cold water, bring to the boil and cook for 1 minute, then run under cold water. When cold, peel and halve. Flake the salmon into a bowl, removing any bones, then season with pepper. Plunge the mange tout and beans into salted boiling water for 2 minutes, then drain. Cook the oyster mushrooms in the olive oil for about 5 minutes or until juicy and tender. Tear the curly endive into small pieces and place on a large, flat serving dish. Arrange the salmon, mange tout, beans, oyster mushrooms and cheese on the endive. Put the quail eggs and cherry tomatoes round the edge, then sprinkle over the pine nuts, if using. Just before serving, pour over the French dressing.

SERVES 12 / ❦❦

Whole Dressed Salmon

Always ask your fishmonger to remove the backbone, because it looks so awful exposed when the top layer has been served on a buffet table. (Ask to keep the head and tail, and cook them in the foil with the fish fillets if you wish to use them as garnish.) You can take off the grey flesh under the skin but I leave it on unless clients ask me to remove it, and most do prefer it left on. I stuff the middle with Herb Mayonnaise (see page 154) and garnish it very scantily, otherwise the bits get in the way when serving.

1 × 2.8 kilo / 6 lb salmon, filleted but skin left on
a little butter
1 lemon, sliced
a few sprigs of fresh parsley
a few sprigs of fresh thyme or oregano (optional)
¼ cucumber, thinly sliced
2 tbsp Herb Mayonnaise (see page 154)

For the garnish:
a few lemon and cucumber slices and sprigs of parsley

Preheat the oven to 180°C/375°F/gas mark 4. Butter a piece of foil large enough to wrap the salmon in. Place one fish half, skin side down, on the foil, lay over some lemon slices, parsley and the sprigs of thyme or oregano, if using. Place the other half of the salmon, skin side up, on top and wrap up well in the foil. Place on a flat baking tray and bake for 30 minutes or until the salmon is just cooked. (Poke the thick end of the flesh with a pointed knife; the flesh should flake easily.) Remove, then leave to cool in its wrapping. When lukewarm, unwrap and carefully peel off the skin, then lift onto a smooth surface. Discard the lemon and herbs from the middle, carefully turn the remaining half over and then peel off the skin. Place the less attractive side on a flat serving dish, spread over some herb mayonnaise, then lay the fillet remaining on top. Garnish with the remaining lemon slices, cucumber slices and sprigs of parsley. Chill until ready to serve.

SERVES 12 / 🍶🍶

Prawn and Almond Roulade

This may sound strange but it is popular with people who like experimenting with flavours. I normally serve it on a buffet table but it also makes a good starter, two thin slices per person served on a bed of mixed leaf salad.

175 g / 6 oz ground almonds
1 tbsp self-raising flour
4 eggs, separated
1 tbsp soft light-brown sugar

For the filling:
225 g / 8 oz prawns, cooked and shelled
2″ piece of cucumber, peeled and finely chopped
¼ red pepper, seeded, cored and finely chopped
½ stick of celery, strings removed, and finely chopped
4 tbsp Mayonnaise (see page 154)
salt and freshly ground black pepper
a little Parmesan, finely grated

Preheat the oven to 180°C/350°F/gas mark 4. Line a roasting tin or grill pan without the wire rack, 35 cm × 27.5 cm / 14″ × 11″, with greaseproof paper. Mix the ground almonds with the flour in a bowl. Put the egg yolks and sugar in a bowl and whisk on

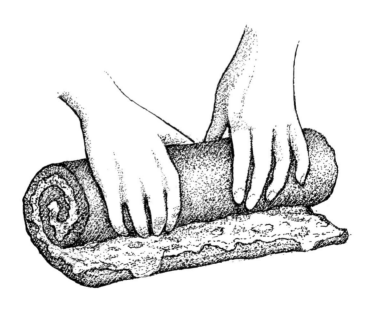

HOW TO ROLL UP

high, adding 3 tbsp boiling water. Whisk for 3 minutes or until light and fluffy. Fold in the almond mixture. Whisk the egg whites in a dry bowl until stiff, then fold into the mixture. Pour into the lined tin and bake for about 10 minutes or until set but not browning. Remove from the tin and leave to cool on the paper. Mix all the filling ingredients in a bowl. Place a clean piece of greaseproof paper on a work surface, sprinkle with Parmesan and tip the cooked roulade onto the clean paper, then peel off the old paper. Spread over the filling mixture right to the edges and roll up, holding the two long ends. Place the roulade on a serving dish and, when ready to serve, slice like a Swiss Roll.

SERVES 8 / ♠♠♠

Grilled Mixed Vegetables

This has suddenly become very trendy in chefs' circles but it has been served in Italy for years. I first came across it when I was working with a Grand Prix team in Sicily and we went to a restaurant that clung to the side of a mountain in the middle of the island. Everything was either cooked on a grill or baked in huge clay ovens. If you can't buy oyster mushrooms, use button mushrooms. Serve with our Corn Bread (see page 151).

1 large aubergine, topped, tailed and sliced
salt and freshly ground black pepper
a little olive oil
1 large onion, peeled and roughly chopped
4 courgettes, topped, tailed and sliced
*125 g	4 oz oyster mushrooms, wiped*
4–5 tomatoes, halved
*1 × 400 g	14 oz tin of artichoke bottoms, drained*
2 red peppers, cored, deseeded and roughly chopped
*50 g	2 oz piece of Parmesan*

Place the aubergine slices in a single layer, sprinkle with salt and leave for 10 minutes, then wash them and pat dry. Heat the grill to high, brush the vegetables with olive oil, season with salt and pepper, then grill in turn until each is cooked, turning once. Layer the vegetables on a serving dish, then grate large curls of Parmesan on the top. Serve warm or cold on a buffet table.

SERVES 8–10 ♠♠

SALADS

Iceberg, Avocado and Kiwi-Fruit Salad

Here is one of our old favourites, easy to make, with its crisp iceberg lettuce contrasting with the smooth texture of avocado and kiwi-fruit. If you wish to prepare it in advance, leave the avocado in the dressing, then add to the salad when ready to serve. Cucumber, fennel, peppers or tomatoes can be added, if wished. Fresh herbs are always a joy to add to any salad and really bring it to life.

1 iceberg lettuce, washed and torn into bite-sized pieces
2 ripe avocados
8 tbsp French Dressing (see page 153)
2 kiwi-fruit, peeled, halved and sliced
1 tbsp freshly chopped mixed herbs, such as parsley, lovage, oregano, mint and basil

Put the lettuce in a salad bowl. Cut the avocados in half and remove the stones. Cut through the flesh but not the skin, 4 cuts lengthways and 6 cuts across. Using a dessertspoon, scoop out the flesh into a small bowl, then mix with the dressing, to prevent the flesh discolouring. Add the lettuce, then add the kiwi-fruit and herbs and toss well. Serve.

SERVES 6–8 / 🍶

Caesar Salad

This is one of my favourites: crunchy lettuce, runny egg and curls of fresh Parmesan make a change from the usual green salad. If you have not got time to make your own croûtons, you can buy them ready-made. Some of the packeted varieties are very good but cut them in half with a sharp knife; this makes them easier to eat and looks more home-made.

3 slices of bread
oil for shallow frying
1 Cos lettuce
4 eggs
*½ 50 g	2 oz tin of anchovy fillets*
French Dressing (see page 153)
*50 g	2 oz block of fresh Parmesan*

Cut the bread into 15 mm / ½″ cubes, shallow fry until golden brown, then place on kitchen roll to drain. Remove the outer leaves of the Cos lettuce, break the rest into bite-sized pieces and put in a salad bowl. Bring a small pan of water to the boil, plunge the eggs in for 1 minute, then run the eggs under cold water. Crack the top open, then scoop out straight into the salad bowl, scraping out the lids of the eggs as well. Chop the anchovy fillets, then, add to the lettuce with the oil from the tin. Add about 4 tbsp French Dressing and the croutons and toss well. Using a coarse grater, grate over the Parmesan cheese in large curls, then serve.

SERVES 8 / 🌢

Spinach Salad

Young, tender spinach leaves are essential. Spinach makes a welcome change from lettuce and has the extra bonus of being very good for you. You can substitute 3 chopped hen's eggs for the quail eggs, and for vegetarians omit the bacon and perhaps add pine nuts.

450 g / 1 lb tender spinach leaves, thoroughly washed
oil for shallow frying
4 rashers of bacon, rindless and cut into strips
3 slices of bread, cut into 15 mm / ½" cubes
12 quail eggs
150 ml / 5 fl oz soured cream
2 tbsp French Dressing (see page 153)

Tear the spinach leaves into bite-sized pieces, then put in a salad bowl. Heat the oil in a frying pan, add the bacon and fry until crisp. Drain. Add the bread cubes, then fry until golden brown all over. Drain. Plunge the quail eggs into boiling water for 2 minutes, then run under cold water, peel then halve. When ready to serve, add the remaining ingredients to the spinach and toss well.

SERVES 6–8 / ♥

Red Salad

This is a pretty salad, with its clash of reds, especially good at Christmas.

½ red cabbage, cored and cut into bite-sized pieces
1 radicchio, washed and torn into bite-sized pieces
1 red pepper, cored, deseeded and cut into bite-sized pieces
1 bunch of radishes, tops removed, then halved
6 tomatoes, cut into bite-sized pieces
125 g / 4 oz seedless red grapes, halved
2 large carrots, peeled and coarsely grated (optional)
50 g / 2 oz sultanas
6–8 tbsp French Dressing (see page 153)

Mix the ingredients together, then dress with the French Dressing when ready to serve.

SERVES 10–12 / ♥

Louisiana Mixed Bean Salad

A great favourite on a buffet table because it adds contrast to leafy salads, this can also be served hot as a vegetable. Most supermarkets now sell packets of mixed dried beans.

*450 g	1 lb mixed dried beans such as flageolets and red kidney beans soaked overnight in water*
salt and freshly ground black pepper
3 tbsp olive oil
1 onion, peeled and finely chopped
1 garlic clove, peeled and crushed
1 tbsp chopped fresh parsley
juice of ½ lemon

Rinse the beans, place in a saucepan of fresh salted water, then boil rapidly, uncovered, for 10 minutes. Reduce the heat, cover and simmer for a further 30–40 minutes, or until tender. Drain. Heat the oil in a frying pan, add the onion and garlic and fry over a low heat for 10 minutes or until the onion is soft but not brown. Leave to cool. Mix the ingredients together and transfer to a serving dish. Chill until ready to serve.

SERVES 6–8 / ♠

Tomato and Mozzarella Salad

Easy, foolproof and fresh. Use big 'beef' tomatoes if possible, otherwise use 16 ordinary ones. The cheese can be bought in most supermarkets, in small bags of whey, which keeps them fresh and wet.

8 large 'beef' tomatoes, sliced
*2 × 200 g	7 oz packets of Mozarella cheese, drained and sliced*
*1 × 200 g	7 oz jar of sun-dried tomatoes in olive oil, drained and chopped very small, oil reserved (optional) or 2 tbsp olive oil*
12–16 fresh basil leaves
*75 g	3 oz pine nuts*
salt and freshly ground black pepper

Arrange the sliced tomatoes and cheese on a serving dish, scatter over the sun-dried tomatoes, if using, then tear up the basil leaves and place over the top, with the pine nuts. Drizzle with the sun-dried tomato oil or olive oil and season well.

SERVES 8–12 / ♠

Carrot and Orange Salad

This has a beautiful colour and is very fresh tasting; you can pour over a little French Dressing (see page 153), if wished, but I prefer the clean flavour without. The coriander is optional; it is not a flavour I like but many people do!

450 g | 1 lb carrots, peeled and grated with a potato peeler
4 medium-sized oranges
1 small bunch of coriander leaves (optional)
1 small bulb of fennel, finely chopped (optional)
1 bunch of watercress, leaves only
juice of ½ lemon
salt and freshly ground black pepper
1 tbsp pine nuts
a little sugar, if necessary

Put the carrots in a salad bowl. Peel the oranges with a sharp knife as you would an apple, removing the pith and skin, and holding them over the bowl to catch the juices. Cut out the segments, remove the pips and add to the carrot and coriander. Add the remaining ingredients and mix well. Chill and serve.

SERVES 8 / ✋

Cucumber and Strawberry Salad

You could serve this light, well-flavoured salad with any of the salmon recipes in this book. Make sure you marinate the cucumbers for an hour or two so that the sweet and sour mixture sinks right through the flesh.

1 large cucumber
salt and freshly ground black pepper
2 tbsp wine vinegar
1 tsp caster sugar
225 g | 8 oz strawberries, hulled and halved

Peel the cucumber with a potato peeler, then slice very thinly. Arrange in a serving dish. Mix the seasoning, vinegar and sugar in a cup, then pour over the cucumbers. Leave for an hour or more to marinate. Arrange the halved strawberries on the cucumber slices and serve chilled.

SERVES 8–10 / ✋

Waldorf Salad

Originally from the Waldorf Astoria Hotel in New York, this fruity, crunchy salad goes well on a winter buffet table and adds contrast to other salads.

225 g / 8 oz chicory, sliced in 15 mm / ½" slices
2 large, red dessert apples, cored and cut into bite-sized pieces
4 sticks of celery, strings removed, washed and chopped
125 g / 4 oz walnuts, chopped
4 tbsp Mayonnaise (see page 154)
salt and freshly ground black pepper

Put the ingredients in a salad bowl and mix well. Chill until ready to serve.

SERVES 8 / 🌶

Pasta Pesto Salad

This is simple and takes only a few minutes to prepare, since you can buy pesto sauce, which is a blend of pine nuts, basil and olive oil, in a jar. Choose any pasta shape you like but read the packet for cooking times if it is dried; fresh pasta takes only about 3 minutes to cook and needs to be watched carefully to guard against overcooking.

450 g / 1 lb pasta shapes
salt and freshly ground black pepper
a few drops of oil
1 tbsp olive oil
2 tbsp pesto sauce
6 tomatoes, each cut into bite-sized pieces
125 g / 4 oz pine nuts (optional)

Plunge the pasta into lots of rapidly boiling salted water with a few added drops of oil, stir well, then cook for the recommended time. Drain in a colander, then tip into a bowl. Mix the olive oil with the pesto, then mix into the pasta. Stir in the tomatoes and season with pepper, and salt if necessary. Transfer to a serving bowl, sprinkle over the pine nuts, then serve.

SERVES 8 / 🌶

Cracked Wheat Salad

Fresh mint and lemon juice are essential, to make this recipe come alive.

*225 g	8 oz Bulgar wheat*
8 spring onions, trimmed and finely chopped
1 tbsp chopped fresh mint
juice of 1 lemon
salt and freshly ground black pepper
4 tbsp olive oil

Put the cracked wheat in a large bowl and pour over 450 ml / 15 fl oz boiling water, or according to packet instructions. Fork through from time to time and leave to cool. Using a fork, mix in the rest of the ingredients. Check the seasoning, then chill until ready to serve.

SERVES 6–8 / ✋

Brown Rice Salad

One of my bêtes noires is currants in a rice salad, so you won't find one here. Feel free, however, to add or omit ingredients as this nutritious salad is versatile. It can be made a day in advance and left to mellow, but add the bananas at the last minute otherwise they go brown. Allow for 25 g / 1 oz uncooked rice per person for rice salad served with several other salads and 50 g / 2 oz uncooked rice per person served with a main course. The onion and clove idea was given to me by Donald Sinden's wife, Diana, and is excellent for any rice to which you wish to impart that 'clovey aroma'.

*225 g	8 oz short-grain brown rice*
6 cloves
1 small onion, peeled
salt and freshly ground black pepper
1 heaped tsp cumin
1 tbsp runny honey
*125 g	4 oz salted peanuts*
¼ cucumber, finely chopped
1 tbsp freshly chopped parsley
1 red pepper, cored, deseeded and finely chopped
1 large banana, peeled and sliced

Push the cloves into the onion, then cook with the rice in salted water according to instructions on the packet. Drain, discard the onion, then place the rice in a bowl. Add the cumin, honey, peanuts, cucumber, parsley, red pepper and black pepper, stir then chill until ready to serve. Add the bananas, mix well, then spoon into a serving bowl.

SERVES 8 / 🖐

Potato Salads

There are many potato salad recipes; here are three with different, mix-and-match dressings. For a buffet, for example, if you serve chicken in mayonnaise, dress the potatoes in vinaigrette to add variety. New potatoes are ready available in most areas all-year-round, but the West Country new potato appears in early May and, to my mind, it can't be beaten for flavour, so don't miss that moment.

'West Country Way' Potato Salad

900 g / 2 lb new potatoes, washed
salt
a little cooking oil
4 rashers of back bacon, rind removed and chopped into strips
1 garlic clove, peeled and chopped (optional)
4 spring onions, washed and finely chopped
4 tbsp Mayonnaise (see page 154)
freshly ground black pepper
1 dsp freshly chopped mint

Cook the potatoes in salted boiling water for about 15 minutes or until just tender when speared with a sharp knife. Drain and leave to cool. Meanwhile, heat the oil and fry the bacon and garlic, if using, in a pan until fairly crisp. Mix all the ingredients together, transfer to a serving dish and chill until ready to serve.

SERVES 6–8 / 🖐

Hot Potato Salad

900 g | 2 lb new potatoes, washed

For the dressing:

4 tbsp French Dressing (see page 153)

1 tbsp mixed chopped parsley and rosemary

Cook the potatoes as above, drain and keep warm. Mix the dressing and herbs, then pour over the warm potatoes. Toss and serve.

SERVES 6–8 / ❦

Soured Cream Potato Salad

900 g | 2 lb new potatoes, washed

For the dressing:

150 ml | 5 fl oz soured cream

1 tsp pesto sauce or 1 bunch of fresh chives

salt and freshly ground black pepper

Cook the potatoes as above, drain and leave to cool. Mix the soured cream, pesto, if using, and pepper in a cup, then pour over the potatoes. Mix well and, if omitting the pesto, snip over the chives. Chill and serve.

SERVES 6–8 / ❦

BREADS

Herb and Garlic Bread

When I serve this at office lunches I leave out the garlic as its after-effects can be antisocial, but in the evenings I make up for it. Fresh herbs definitely taste much better but the dried do perfectly well.

*125 g	4 oz butter, softened*
1 garlic clove, peeled and crushed
1 dsp mixed, chopped herbs such as thyme, parsley and oregano
1 long French stick

Preheat the oven to 200°C/400°F/gas mark 6. Put the butter, garlic and herbs in a small bowl and mix well with a round-bladed knife. Cut the French stick in 2.5 cm / 1″ slices, nearly but not quite all the way through. Spread the butter generously between each slice, making sure the loaf stays intact, then wrap well with foil. If it is too long for the oven, make 2 parcels. Bake for about 15 minutes or until the butter is melted.

SERVES 6–10 / 🌢 / FREEZE

Corn Bread

My mum was brought up on this bread in America (she was allowed a few other foods too!) and we still have plenty in the house. It is particularly good with a starter but also at tea-time.

*175 g	6 oz yellow cornmeal*
*175 g	6 oz self-raising flour*
1 good dsp caster sugar
4 tsp baking powder
½ tsp salt
*125 g	4 oz butter*
*300 ml	10 fl oz skimmed milk*
1 large egg, beaten

Preheat the oven to 190°C/375°F/gas mark 5. Mix the dry ingredients in a bowl, then rub in the butter with your fingertips or use a blender until the mixture resembles breadcrumbs. Add the milk and egg; mix with a spoon. Put into a 450 g / 1 lb non-stick loaf tin and bake for 45 minutes or until well risen and slightly brown on top. Test by inserting a skewer in the centre; it should come out clean. Turn out and serve warm.

SERVES 8 / 🌢 / FREEZE

Delphi Lodge Bread

I often go salmon and sea trout fishing at a little place called Leenane in County Mayo, Ireland. I never have much luck fishing, although I am told I have a promising 'cast', but my big find was the recipe for this loaf. I have never tasted better and we sell out in our shop almost before it has come out of the oven. You can make larger quantities and freeze the extra, but as it is so easy to make, try to make it and eat it straight from the oven. The ingredients are easiest bought in a health shop.

175 g | 6 oz wholemeal flour
50 g | 2 oz self-raising flour
50 g | 2 oz pinhead oatmeal
50 g | 2 oz wheatgerm
50 g | 2 oz bran
1 tsp baking soda
¼ tsp salt
1 tsp sugar
1 egg
300 ml | 10 fl oz skimmed milk
sunflower seeds (optional)

Preheat the oven to 190°C/375°F/gas mark 5. Place the dry ingredients in a large bowl and mix well. Add the egg and milk and mix well with a spoon. Put into a 450 g / 1 lb non-stick loaf tin, roughly even out the top, sprinkle over the sunflower seeds, if wished, and bake for 45–60 minutes or until crisp and a skewer inserted in the middle comes out clean.

SAUCES AND DRESSINGS

French Dressing

Dressing is as important for a salad as for a human being! Without it, both can be very dull-looking, though of course there are exceptions. And with both, taste is such a personal thing that you must adjust the final result to suit yourself. If you prefer the flavour on the sharp side, add more vinegar, if you prefer it sweeter, add more sugar. I make the dressing in a measuring jug, for convenience, but it can be made and kept in a bottle, for a month or more, to use any time. Remember to give it a good shake before pouring.

1 garlic clove, peeled and crushed
1 tsp mustard powder or coarse-grain mustard
1 tsp paprika
a pinch of curry powder
salt and freshly ground black pepper
2 tsp caster sugar
1 tsp dried oregano
1 tsp thyme
juice of 1 lemon
*50 ml	2 fl oz cider or sherry vinegar*
*300 ml	10 fl oz olive oil*

Put all the ingredients except the lemon juice, vinegar and oil into a jug and mix well. Add the lemon juice and stir well. Add the vinegar and oil and whisk. Adjust the taste and serve.

Mayonnaise

There is no substitute for home-made mayonnaise, but if you have to compromise, add lemon juice, freshly ground black pepper and mustard to a good bought brand. This recipe will keep, refrigerated, for 1–2 weeks. I find that an electric hand whisk mixes the egg yolks better than a blender does. Add the first drops of oil very slowly, to prevent curdling, but if the mixture does curdle, don't panic. Put 2 egg yolks into a bowl and slowly whisk the curdled mixture back into the new egg yolks and all should be well. For Herb Mayonnaise, add a handful of finely chopped thyme, oregano, basil and parsley and stir well.

2 large egg yolks
½ tsp mustard powder
1 tsp caster sugar
*300 ml	10 fl oz olive oil*
1 tbsp wine vinegar
1 tbsp lemon juice
salt and freshly ground black pepper

Put the egg yolks, mustard and sugar in a bowl just large enough for the oil or in a blender and whizz well. Then very gradually add the oil in the thinnest stream possible. When half is added, add the vinegar to thin the mixture, then slowly add the rest of the oil, whisking on high again. Whisk in the lemon juice and season with salt and pepper. Put into a jug and keep chilled.

❦❦

Cold Watercress Hollandaise

This is a lovely change from mayonnaise, ideal with cold salmon, and is not hard to make. For traditional, warm Hollandaise, serve it after pouring in the butter, or keep in a thermos for an hour or two until ready to serve. A blender or liquidiser is essential for this quick method; it can be made a day in advance and kept chilled.

*225 g	8 oz salted butter*
3 egg yolks
juice of 1 lemon
freshly ground black pepper
*300 ml	10 fl oz soured cream*
1 bunch of watercress, stalks removed

Put the butter in a small saucepan, ideally with a pouring lip, then melt over a low heat. Put the egg yolks, lemon juice and black pepper in a blender or liquidiser. When the butter has melted bring to a high boil, turn on he blender on liquidiser to high, then pour the bubbling butter at a steady speed into the egg yolk mixture. Blend for 30 seconds. Cool slightly, add the soured cream and watercress, then blend for a few seconds more. Pour into a bowl and serve or chill and serve later.

SERVES 8 / ♥♥

Chicken Stock

If you have a freezer the easiest way to make chicken stock is not when you need it but whenever you have a chicken carcass left. After stripping the flesh, put the carcass and whichever vegetables you have from the list below in a pot. Simmer for a few hours, cool, then freeze. Just remove from the freezer a few hours before using.

1 chicken carcass
1 onion, quartered
2 carrots, peeled and cut into large pieces
1 stick of celery, washed and cut into large pieces
1 leek, washed and cut into large pieces
1 bouquet garni or mixed fresh herbs
salt and freshly ground black pepper

Put all the ingredients in a large saucepan, add water to cover and bring to the boil. Cover, then simmer for 2 hours, topping up with more water if necessary. Leave to cool and then strain. Remove the fat from the top with a large spoon. Store in a refrigerator for up to 2 days or freeze until ready to use.

♥ / FREEZE

Cumberland Sauce

This sauce is delicious with roast gammon or cold sliced ham, lamb chops or game pies. It can be kept, refrigerated, in a sealed jar for a week or two so double the quantities, for convenience.

2 tbsp redcurrant jelly
grated rind and juice of ½ lemon
grated rind and juice of 1 orange
1 tbsp port

Put all the ingredients except the port in a small saucepan, then gently heat, breaking the jelly into small pieces. Keep over low heat until the jelly melts completely, then add the port. Leave to cool, then store in a sealed jar or serve cold.

SERVES 6–8 / 🍶

Index